MICHAEL PARKINSON
ON FOOTBALL

Also by Michael Parkinson

Michael Parkinson on Golf
Football Daft
Cricket Mad
Sporting Fever
Bats in the Pavilion
Best – An Intimate Biography
A–Z of Soccer
The Woofits
Parkinson's Lore
The Best of Parkinson
Sporting Lives
Sporting Profiles

About the Author

Michael Parkinson began his career as a journalist on the *Manchester Guardian*. He started writing about sport for the *Observer* and wrote a column for the *Sunday Times* for fifteen years. His legendary chatshow *Parkinson* is currently back on the BBC with huge success. He also hosts *Parkinson's Sunday Supplement* on Radio Two and writes a regular column for the *Daily Telegraph*.

MICHAEL PARKINSON

ON FOOTBALL

Michael Parkinson

Illustrated by John Ireland

coronet

CORONET BOOKS
Hodder & Stoughton

Copyright © 2001 by Michael Parkinson

First published in Great Britain in 2002
by Hodder and Stoughton
A division of Hodder Headline

The right of Michael Parkinson to be identified as the Author of
the Work has been asserted by him in accordance with the
Copyright, Designs and Patents Act 1988.

A Coronet paperback

2 4 6 8 10 9 7 5 3 1

A CIP catalogue record for this title is available
from the British Library

ISBN 0 340 82107 8

Typeset in Sabon by
Rowland Phototypesetting Ltd,
Bury St Edmunds, Suffolk
Printed and bound in Great Britain by
Clays Ltd, St Ives plc

Hodder and Stoughton
A division of Hodder Headline
338 Euston Road
London NW1 3BH

Contents

CONTENTS

INTRODUCTION

This compilation covers a lifetime of watching football and was made with great foreboding on my part. Journalism is not meant to exist beyond the moment it endeavours to explain. Its only other purpose is to provide the wrapping for fish and chips.

Moreover, it can be depressing laying out your life – or at least a significant part of it – in a line of long-forgotten articles. It serves as a reminder of the gap between ambition and achievement, throws up examples of work that is awkward or flowery or both.

While chronicling the changes in the game over the years the compilation can also indicate the fluctuating personality and mood of the writer. Did that funny young lad really become that sour grouch? Did he change naturally or was it the game to blame? As ever, the reader will decide.

When it came to choosing what to include and to leave out I handed responsibility to my good friend Roddy Bloomfield who published my first books on sport way back in the sixties. I am glad he included some of the early writing about growing up in a Yorkshire village and watching Barnsley as a child. My grandchildren will never know what a miner looked like, nor the kind of society their grandparents came from. The memories of my childhood might give them a clue. For my own part, they remind me how blessed

I was to be born of loving parents in a community that shared everything, including and mostly laughter.

The introduction to this collection was written for a book published thirty years ago. It sums up my feelings today. That much has not changed.

*　　*　　*

I was five years old when I was taken to my first game of football. My father reminds me occasionally that at half-time when he asked me how I liked it I said, 'It's all right but I think we'll go now.' To which he replied, 'I don't think we will,' thereby making a decision which condemned me to a lifetime of addiction to the game. Out of that first tentative encounter grew a love affair which has lasted until the present without showing the slightest sign of weakening. The name of the lady is Barnsley and through the years – the few good ones, the many lean ones – I have loved her like my favourite barmaid. Even now it's easy to switch my mind back to the days when we caught the bus and made the five-mile journey into Barnsley to see the Reds play. It was always crowded with men in hairy overcoats and flat caps, smelling of Woodbines and last night's beer. At the station we would join the chattering throng as it surged up the hill and down the dip to the ground. Oakwell, the home of Barnsley Football Club, could not by any stretch of the imagination be called a pleasant spot, but no sight has thrilled me more, before or since, than the sudden view of the ground as we breasted the hill from the bus station and our eyes met the place where our heroes lived. Even now their names are easily remembered, like some familiar prayer: Binns, Harston, Shotton, Logan, Birkenshaw, Asquith, Smith, Cooling, Robledo, Barlow and McGarry. Inside the ground we would head for our favourite spot, to the east of the players' entrance on the terrace. It had been my father's spot since he got a rise at the pit which enabled him to move from the back of the goals.

There we would be joined, week in week out, by our little but noisy family of regulars. There was the Maniac, charmingly called because of his towering outbursts of rage which occurred every time the opposition committed a foul. And Wobblygob, a spotty youth who earned his name through a pair of exceptionally full lips. This unfortunate act of nature was remarked most cruelly one Saturday by a Rotherham fan, who, tiring of the abuse being heaped on his team, turned round and said, 'Tha' could ride a bike round thi' gob.'

Together we shared the infinite pleasures and black despair which any football fan goes through following the fortunes of his team. It was in that same spot, with the view of the muck stacks on the other side, that I stood and saw many things beautiful and ugly, sad and comic, and every Saturday grew more in love with the game. It was here that I first saw Frank Swift, massive and graceful, explain the art of goalkeeping. I remember vividly Swift catching the ball with one hand and holding it above the head of a tiny Barnsley forward who kept jumping for it like a dog for a bone. It was here I saw a stripling youth called Blanchflower spin the first delicate lines of his genius and looking as incongruous as a thoroughbred in a donkey derby. Here too I saw Matthews and Doherty and Carter and Lawton and Mortensen and Shackleton. But great as they were, and glamorous too, I never loved them as much as the nondescripts who made up the Barnsley team throughout the years.

Watching football today I am constantly aware of the changes that have taken place, not so much in the game itself but in the actual physical appearance of the men who play it. Today's young men are sleek and streamlined. If you line them up there's nothing in their appearance to tell you who is the right full-back and who is the inside-right. When I first watched football, every player was built according to his position. The goalkeeper was always a light heavyweight, muscular but not muscle-bound. The full-backs were short, squat men with prison hair-cuts, no-nonsense faces and fearsome legs. The centre-half was always the tallest man in the side, with a forehead hammered flat through contact with a thousand muddy footballs, and flanking him were the wing-halves, the frighteners, who were invariably built on the lines of dance-hall bouncers. The right-wing was always small and fast, the left-wing bandy-legged and tricky, the centre-forward wore the desperate, haunted look of a man who was expected to run through brick walls and be roundly abused if he shirked it. The inside-forwards invariably wore their hair a little longer than the rest and carried with them an air of intellectual superiority, like grammar school boys playing in a pit team.

Throughout the years, every Saturday afternoon when it always seemed to be raining, this united collection of assorted human beings decided my mood for the coming week. If they won we went home chattering with excitement and the old man took my mother to the boozer and I'd go to the cinema. If they lost, the trek to the bus station was like a funeral cortège, the bus was a hearse and the report in that night's *Green 'Un* an obituary to a loved one.

I last stood on that spot on the terrace in Barnsley a couple of years ago and since that time have seen football in many places. I have seen Real Madrid in Spain, Milan in Italy, I have travelled to games by gondola, air-conditioned Cadillac and private light aeroplane. But I have never got over Barnsley. Once in Los Angeles I picked up an American paper which in small print said Barnsley 1, Stockport County 21, and I spent three worried days and sleepless nights until the rice-paper editions arrived to tell me that there had been a misprint and the game had been drawn.

There are, of course, thousands more like me; all I have done is to describe a symptom known to every man who ever gave his heart to a football team. I am luckier than most in that my therapy is in being allowed to write what I remember. This book is one man's very personal view of football. Some went to soccer simply to stand for ninety minutes in the open air as a welcome change to a lifetime spent underground; others went to rid their frustration on someone who couldn't hit back; some like myself went because we were caught in a daft love affair which defied reason but gave us colour, movement, humour, drama and a million memories.

What follows are mainly memories, the rest are daydreams, and a few gripes.

BACKYARD
ODDBALLS

Necessary screwballs

GOALKEEPERS, like things that go bump in the night, defy analysis. They are as much a mystery in the general order of things as the function of the human appendix. It is, of course, relatively easy to explain what they have to do: their purpose is to prevent the ball entering the net by any means at their disposal, namely by catching it, punching it, kicking it, heading it or, if they so desire, throwing their caps at it. The mystery lies in the fact that this seemingly simple, straightforward task produces people of incredibly complex and often eccentric personality. Even today, when the game appears to be played by robots, when individuality is ruthlessly stifled at birth, the goalkeeper has survived with all his personal idiosyncrasies intact. No one knows better than goalkeepers themselves that the price they pay for their freedom is to be talked about behind their backs. In the totalitarian regime of modern-day soccer they are treated as necessary screwballs. Because of this, it is a commonly held belief that all goalkeepers have a slate loose, that the nature of the job being what it is a man must be barmy to do it. The other theory is that the goalkeeper, because he is custodian of the most important part of a football field, slowly develops into a paranoiac.

I suspect that Clakker May would be regarded as a classic example by those people who reckon all goalkeepers are born crazy. You'd never suspect there was anything wrong by looking at him. He was a tall, stringy, quiet youth who lived with his parents and ten brothers and sisters in a council house near the pit gates. He became our goalkeeper quite by chance. One day we were a man short, and Len, our trainer, asked Clakker to play in goal. The result was a revelation. It wasn't so much that when he donned the jersey he changed in his attitude towards his team-mates, it was simply that he believed that the rules of the game related to everyone except himself.

We became aware of his quirk the first time he touched the ball. He left his goalline to meet a hard, high cross, caught the ball cleanly, shaped to clear downfield, and then, for no apparent reason, spun round and fled to the back of the net. This move dumbfounded players, officials and spectators alike. As we stood gaping, Clakker ran from the back of the net and booted the ball over the halfway line. Nobody moved as it bounced aimlessly towards the opposite goal and then the referee broke the silence by blowing on his whistle and pointing to the centre spot. This appeared to upset Clakker.

'What's tha' playin' at?' he asked the referee.

'I was just about to ask thee same question,' said the referee. By this time Len had run on to the field.

'What the bloody hell . . .' he began.

'Nay, Len. Tha' sees I caught this ball and then I looks up and I saw this big centre forrard coming at me and I thought, "Bugger this lot", so I got out of his way,' Clakker explained.

'Tha' ran into t'bloody net wi' t'ball and tha' scoored,' Len shouted.

'Scoored,' said Clakker, incredulously.

'Scoored,' said Len, emphatically.

Clakker shook his head. Len tried to keep calm. 'Look, lad,' he said, putting his arm round Clakker's shoulders, 'I know it's thi' first game and all that, but tha' must get one thing straight. When tha' catches t'ball gi' it some clog downfield. Whatever tha' does don't run into t'net.'

Clakker nodded.

But it made little difference. In the next twenty minutes Clakker ran into the net thirteen times and we were losing 14–2. At this point the referee intervened. He called us all together and said: 'Na' look, lads, this is making mock of a great game. If it goes on like this t'scoor will be in t'hundreds and I'll have to mek a repoort to t'League Management Committee and there'll be hell to play.' We all nodded in agreement. The referee thought a bit and then said:

'What we'll do is amend t'rules. If Clakker runs into t'back of t'net in future it won't count as a goal, allus providin' he caught t'ball on t'right side of t'line in t'first place.'

Everyone agreed and play continued with this extraordinary amendment to the rules. At the final whistle we had lost fifteen to five and Clakker had shown that apart from his eccentric interpretation of the rules he was a remarkably good goalkeeper. Nobody said much after the game. It seemed useless to ask Clakker what went wrong because all of us agreed that like all goalkeepers he was a bit screwy. Our theory was confirmed by Clakker's old man, who when told of his son's extraordinary behaviour simply shook his head and said, 'He allus was a bit potty.'

But that was not the end of Clakker's career, not quite. He was picked for the next game because we didn't want to hurt him too much. Len, the trainer, called us together on the night before the game and explained how we might curb Clakker's madness. His plan was that the defenders should close in behind Clakker whenever he went out for a ball and bar his way into the net. Any resistance from Clakker should be firmly dealt with and if possible the ball taken from him and cleared upfield. In case Clakker should break through his own rearguard Len had taken the precaution of hiding the nets. His theory was that provided Clakker ran into goal, but straight out again, the referee would be unable to decide what had happened.

The reports of our last game had attracted a large crowd to the ground for Clakker's second appearance. All his family were present to see if it was true what people were saying about Clakker's extraordinary behaviour.

Things worked quite well for a time. Everytime Clakker caught the ball we fell in around him and urged him away from his goal. Once he escaped us and nipped into goal, but he had the sense to escape immediately around the goalpost and clear downfield. The referee looked puzzled for a minute and gave Clakker a peculiar look, but did not give a goal because he could not believe what he thought he saw. We were leading two goals to nil with five minutes of the first half left when Clakker gave the game away. Over-confident at having duped the referee once before, he ran over his own goalline with the ball. His plan came to grief when he collided with the iron stanchion at the back of the goal. As he staggered drunkenly against the support the referee blew for a goal and gave Clakker the sort of look that meant all was now revealed.

When half-time came none of us could look forward to the next forty-five minutes with any optimism. Len came on the field and beckoned myself and the centre-half to one side.

'Na' look, lads, we've got to do something about yon Clakker,' he said. 'I've thought about playing him out of goal, but that's too dangerous. I can't just take him off because yon referee wouldn't allow it. So there's only one thing we can do.' He paused and looked at both of us.

'What's that?' I asked.

'Fix him,' said Len.

'Fix him?' I said. Len nodded.

'When you get a chance, and as soon as you can, clobber him. I don't want him to get up, either,' said Len.

The centre-half was smiling.

'Look,' I said to him, 'we can't clobber our own team-mate. It's not done.'

He looked at me pityingly.

'Leave it to me,' he said. 'I've fixed nicer people than Clakker.'

It took two minutes of the second half for Clakker to get fixed. There was a scrimmage in our goalmouth and when the dust had cleared Clakker lay prostrate on his goalline. Len came running on to the field, trying to look concerned. The centre-half was trying hard to look innocent. Clakker's father had drifted over to the scene and was looking down at his son's body. 'He's better like that,' he said.

Len said to him, 'Tek your Clakker home and don't let him out till t'game's finished.'

Clakker's old man nodded and signalled to some of his sons to pick Clakker up. The last we saw of them they were carrying Clakker out of the field and home. We did quite well without him and managed to win. Afterwards in the dressing room some of the lads were wondering how Clakker became injured. Len said: 'Tha' nivver can tell wi' goalkeepers. It's quite likely he laid himself out.'

Clakker had a profound effect on me. Since that day many years ago when he was persuaded out of the game, I have never been able to watch a football match without spending a great deal of the time wondering what was going on underneath the goalkeeper's cap. None of the goalkeepers I have ever seen in first-class football could hold a candle to Clakker, but most of them from time to time have revealed flashes of rare individuality. Bradford Park Avenue once had a goalkeeper called Chick Farr who thought nothing of racing far out of his goal area, tackling an opposing forward and racing off downfield like a demented Stanley Matthews. Whenever his little fantasy was interrupted by a successful tackle, Farr would gallop back to his goalline, from time to time casting fearful glances over his shoulder like a man being pursued by a ghost. Farr's other party piece was strictly illegal. When he could not be bothered to save a high shot he would reach nonchalantly above his head and pull the crossbar down. Faced with the inevitable telling off from a referee, Farr would pull his cap down over his eyes and try his best to look gormless. His act was a convincing one, not because he was born that way, but because like every goalkeeper he had become expert in hiding his folly.

Occasionally, however, the stresses of the occupation become too much for some goalkeepers and they crack up. Sometimes it happens in public, as with the recent case of a First Division goalkeeper who showed his displeasure at the way the crowd was criticising his goalkeeping by taking his shorts down and showing a large part of his backside to the terraces. At least this particular goalkeeper relieved himself in one great, spectacular gesture. The majority of his kind spend years suffering between the posts, whipping boys for the mob at the back of the goal, sacrifices to the inefficiency of their team-mates. I watched one goalkeeper at Barnsley suffer this way through many seasons. He came to the club fit and virile and stuffed with confidence. When he left on a free transfer, he had shrunk inside his green jersey, his nerves were destroyed, and it was even rumoured that his wife had left him. I often wondered what became of him and discovered the truth sometime later when I was doing a story about a building site. I was talking football with the foreman when he asked me if I remembered

the goalkeeper. I said I did and the foreman said he was working on the site.

'Where is he?' I asked.

'Up theer,' said the foreman, pointing towards heaven.

'Where exactly,' I enquired, hoping he wasn't trying to be funny.

'On top of yon chimney,' said the foreman.

I peered up, and there, high in the sky, sitting on top of the chimney was the goalkeeper.

'He seems to like it up theer. Can't get him down until it's knockin'-off time,' said the foreman.

I thought there might be a story in it, so I asked the foreman if I might interview the goalkeeper. He shrugged.

'He's a funny bugger, but I'll try.'

He cupped his hands to his mouth and bellowed at the top of the chimney, '*Alf, theer's a repoorter down 'ere who wants to interview thi abart goalkeepin'.*'

There was a long silence. Nothing stirred on the top of the chimney for a while and then the figure turned and looked down. And down the miles of silence separating us floated the reply:

'Tell him to get stuffed.'

The foreman shrugged and said, 'I told you. He's a rum feller. Still, I always think tha's got to be a bit strange to be a goalkeeper.'

I've often wondered since what kind of peace the goalkeeper discovered on top of that chimney, and wondered also what kind of revenge he was planning on the people below who had driven him there. I don't think he was potty or excessively anti-social. It was simply that he, like every goalkeeper, knew what it was like to be one of the world's most abused minority group.

CLOSET WINGERS

IT IS AN AXIOM of the modern game of football that wingmen, like people who thatch roofs and make clogs, are a dying breed. It is remarkable that a country whose one certain contribution to the international history of football is Stanley Matthews should now seem intent on pretending that he never existed.

Once upon a time in the days when footballers wore shorts to their knees and were shod in boots with bulging toe-caps, the sight of the wingman improvising his talents down the touchline, delighting and disappointing in turn, was a commonplace on the football fields of Britain. Wingmen were the temperamental artists whose performance was controlled by the state of the moon, or the horoscope in that morning's *Daily Mirror* or more simply by the fact of whether or not they felt like playing well. They were the only members of a side who were allowed the luxury of personal eccentricity by the fans. I once played with a winger who wore a flat cap and woollen mittens on days when the weather was bad. Neither his team-mates, opponents nor spectators ever remarked his curious attire because he was a wingman. Had he been a centre-half or a full-back he would immediately have been marked down as a weirdo of some sort and asked to mend his ways or retire from the game.

In those dear departed days, the best wingmen were

always referred to as closet wingers. It grew out of the days when we had the best team in the Barnsley and District Backyard League. Our success depended mainly on an unbeaten home record which was achieved by the efforts of our right-winger, Albert, and a long row of outside toilets or closets as they were more commonly known.

Albert was an absolute master at charging down the wing and, when challenged by the opposing defenders, flicking the ball against the toilet door and collecting the rebound. The only time he was known to fail was on the occasion when the occupant of the toilet opened the door in time to take one of Albert's passes in the midriff.

Albert became well known locally as Geronimo, the closet winger. The Geronimo tag had nothing to do with his footballing ability but derived from his hatred of water and hair-cuts which created an appearance to remind us all of the Indians we saw on the screen at the local flea-pit. In those days our tactics were simple and effective. At every conceivable opportunity we would feed the ball to Geronimo, who was invariably lurking by his beloved closets, and away he would go, flicking the ball against the toilet doors, racing on to the rebound and repeating the act until he had cleared the whole defence.

For a couple of seasons we were unbeatable and Albert the closet winger became a local personality. Inevitably it couldn't last for ever and the slide downhill for both Albert and the team came on the day we met

the Klondyke. The team was so named because the part of the village it represented put one in mind of a frontier town during the gold-rush. To describe them as hard opponents would be doing them an injustice. Ferocious is a more accurate description. They had at least two players who would make Mr Norbert Stiles and Señor Rattin look like a pair of cream puffs.

It must also be remembered that in the Backyard League there was no referee to penalise dirty play. The simple ethic therefore was: 'If kicked say nothing, but wait and kick back.' Also in these games we did without the normal post-match formalities like shaking hands and congratulating the other chap. Any team which beat the fearsome Klondyke realised that when the game ended the sensible tactic was to race home immediately because any attempt at the normal courtesies would undoubtedly mean a free ride to the local out-patients department.

It was in this frame of mind we began our epic encounter. All went reasonably well until Albert began his first run down the wing. In and out of the defence he went, flicking the ball on to the toilet doors, the rebound magically dropping at his twinkling feet. With

the Klondyke defence nonplussed, he shot home the first goal.

The Klondyke team, for all the fact that it included many players with surprisingly narrow foreheads and close-set eyes, were not short on swift answers when faced with a problem like this. The next time Albert set off on one of his runs, we were made aware of the Klondyke genius for tactical improvisation. As Albert twinkle-toed along the toilets, the Klondyke full-back, built like a brick brewery, began a diagonal run towards him. As he reached Albert he didn't stop to challenge, he didn't hesitate to decide which way the winger was going, he just kept running as if his target was somewhere on the horizon beyond Albert's right shoulder. The noise of impact, of bone on bone, was terrible, and followed immediately by the sound of splintering wood as Albert, the full-back and the ball smashed through one of the green toilet doors. We peered inside and the wreckage was awful.

Albert and the full-back lay at peace on the floor, surrounded by fragments of wood and jagged pieces of what is politely termed sanitary ware. We picked them up and revived them and then had to abandon the match because the owner of the toilet turned up on his daily visit and when he saw the damage went to fetch the police. We never played there again because the law warned us off and some time later the council pulled the toilets down along with the houses they belonged to. The inhabitants were shipped out to a new estate with inside toilets and a better view of the pit. Albert

went with his parents to the new estate, but he was never the same winger without a row of closets. After a couple of months in his new environment Albert went into premature retirement in a remand home for stealing lead. But he had made his mark. Whenever we saw a good winger he was always a 'closet winger'.

It is easy to scoff at closet wingers, but in fact they have made a colourful contribution to our game. What is more significant, it was a closet winger who unwittingly decided the future of English football. As is generally known, it was Sir Alf Ramsey who killed off the old romantic notion of wingmen. In Ramsey's team of workers there was no place for the eccentric or the whimsical. It was a beautiful machine and it didn't need adorning with frills. Now contrary to general opinion, Sir Alf's plan for wingmen did not occur because he simply happened to think about it one day while taking a bath. It is my theory that his scheme for the liquidation of wingmen had lurked in his mind for some considerable time and had its roots in some kind of deep emotional upset – which is where a closet winger called Johnny Kelly comes in.

He was a left-winger of genius who played for Barnsley in the early fifties, a shy, square, sturdy man with the slightly bandy legs that are the hallmark of all great wingers.

I don't know if you've ever considered the remarkable fact that bandy legs are an asset to most sportsmen. That they help people who ride horses is a thought too obvious to need explanation. But it is not generally known that they greatly assist cricketers also. I once played in a cricket team with a man who possessed the most splendid pair of hooped legs I have yet seen.

As a batsman he was particularly skilled in the art of back play. Now this technique was generally suicidal in the league in which we played where the umpires worked strictly to licensing hours and granted leg-before-wicket appeals with increasing regularity as opening time approached. In this situation my bandy-legged friend was the only batsman in the league to play back and prosper. Whenever struck on his superbly bowed legs and appealed against he would simply point to the gap between his limbs, through which all three stumps were clearly visible, and say to the umpire in his most pained voice 'Leg before wicket with a pair of bloody legs like mine?' No umpire, no matter how thirsty, dare give him out!

I digress only in the interests of science and humanity. It is time someone pointed out the virtues of playing sport on a pair of bandy legs. No one who has them should feel unhappy so long as they always remember to play back – which returns us to Alf Ramsey, because those of you with long memories will doubtless recall

that he also used to play back – full-back, that is – and very good he was too. But he was no good against bandy-legged wingers, as Johnny Kelly proved. Kelly was the kind of winger you don't see around nowadays, a player of skill and original wit; the sort of wingman who exploded theories, not expounded them. He played only once for Scotland, which was an act of criminal neglect for a player who must have been the best Scottish winger of his day. That he was ignored has obviously to do with the fact that he played for Barnsley. The selectors in Glasgow obviously thought they played in the Isthmian League – a great pity, because he had unique skill that should have been spread before multitudes and not just the faithful 15,000 who used to watch Barnsley in his day.

Still, it does mean that there were 14,999 other people who will swear to what I am going to tell you now. They and I were present that important day, many years ago, when Alf Ramsey suffered the trauma that changed his life and put the skids under wingers. He was playing right-back for Southampton at the time, an urbane, immaculate footballer who seemed as out of place at Barnsley as a bowler hat in a pawnshop.

In this particular game Johnny Kelly had one of those days when all his genius flowed into his feet. If you have ever seen Matthews or Finney or Georgie Best at their finest then you'll know what I mean. He flicked his hips and Ramsey sat down in wonderment. He waved his foot over the ball like a wand, daring Ramsey to guess what might happen next, and as the full-back anticipated a move outside, Kelly came inside and left him for dead. At one stage he demonstrated his complete mastery by beating Ramsey, waiting for him to recover and then beating him again. Had Kelly been on the Southampton side and doing this to certain of the Barnsley defenders he would have had his impudence rewarded with a bed in the nearest emergency ward. But Ramsey played it clean and endeavoured to look as dignified as any man can when he is having his nose rubbed in the dirt.

The crowd didn't help. They relished the sight of Kelly shredding Ramsey's reputation. This, remember, was in the days when footballers were the victims of individual abuse and not the collective sort they get from today's rehearsed choirs. Thus the comments, though not so loud, were more personal and biting. As Ramsey sat down before Kelly's skill a man near me bellowed, 'Tha' wants to learn how to stand up before tha' plays this game, Ramsey.' And again, as Kelly left Ramsey immobile and helpless as a statue, the same man bawled, 'Ramsey, tha' art about as much use as a chocolate teapot.'

This is as much as any man can be expected to take without consulting the Director of Public Prosecutions. My theory is that as Alf Ramsey sat in that dressing room in Barnsley, scraping the mud from his boots and his reputation, he first thought of his revenge on wingers. He didn't want just Kelly's scalp, but the destruction of the whole tricky race.

It's not a bad theory, particularly when you consider

that Alf Ramsey is where he is today, and Johnny Kelly was last heard of manufacturing a liquid bleach. It's an even stronger theory when you realise that wingers like Kelly are now more rare than five-legged giraffes.

But I have cornered whatever consolation there is left to people who loved the game in the dear, daft days before Mr Ramsey got his paws on it. When I read of the experts trying to explain to themselves just what he is up to, and why, I sit there giggling gently to myself, nursing my memories, thinking fondly of a grey afternoon many seasons ago when a closet winger with bandy legs and baggy shorts made a monkey of a mastermind.

THE UNLOVED ONES

IN THE EVER-CHANGING game of soccer, the lot of the referee remains the same. It is not a happy one. I have always felt sorry for referees because the job they are expected to carry out is basically impossible.

If they are to do their work properly they have to be able to keep close to the ball throughout the ninety minutes of play, a task calling for colossal stamina. At the same time they are expected to make crucial and often very difficult decisions after chasing 100 yards in even time. Those of you who have run 100 yards in ten seconds, only to be met at the tape by a man from N.O.P. who wants to know what you think about the Common Market, will understand what I mean.

Moreover, the referee has also to contend with the baying of a hostile crowd, and the tantrums and snide remarks of the players – and all this for a few bob. Referees know they are not loved except by those nearest and dearest to them. I once saw a referee at Barnsley knocked out by a heavy muddy ball, and as he lay still and forlorn on the ground and the trainer ran across the pitch towards him, someone shouted, 'Don't revive him, bury the sod.' The rest of the crowd agreed.

The position of the referee in the modern game is probably worse than it has ever been. It is the classic example of responsibility without power. They are continually exhorted to get tougher with the players,

and yet when they send off a persistent offender they know that the stiffest sentence the player will receive is a piffling £100 fine and a measly twenty-eight-day suspension.

But whatever happens to improve the lot of the referee, nothing will change his place in society. He will always be unloved by the majority of the population, and will inevitably find it necessary to walk through places like Liverpool with his collar up and his hat brim down, for fear of being recognised. The referee will always occupy that unenviable position of being one who dispenses justice and yet expects none in return.

The saddest example of the referee's plight that I know happened some time ago. His name was Ron and he worked in an office, which fact did not endear him to the majority of players he was expected to control every Saturday afternoon. Where I lived anyone with a white-collar job was a bit suspect.

Ron was the referee one day in a local derby game between our village and a team from two miles down the road. This was a fixture in which traditionally there was a lot of bloodletting. Rivalries were fierce and a few punch-ups were an accepted part of the event. The two main protagonists were our full-back called Blackie and their right-winger called Charlie Onions.

Charlie Onions was completely bald and shy about it, so he used to play in a flat cap. The only time he removed his cap was on the odd occasion when he headed a ball and the more frequent occasions when he was involved in a punch-up. During a fight Charlie's cap became a fearsome weapon. He would fold it so that only the peak showed and then use it to belabour his opponent. The moments when Charlie removed his cap in anger were eagerly awaited by his supporters, who would encourage him with cries of 'Gi' him some bloody neb, Charlie'.

Blackie, on the other hand, was quieter, but just as deadly. He was one of those footballers who never said a word, never squealed if you fouled him, but simply awaited the opportunity to get his own back. Always his revenge was swift and terrible. His battles with Charlie Onions were legendary and eagerly anticipated by the crowd.

On the day of the match, Ron, the referee, made it obvious that, tradition or not, he wasn't going to have any monkey business. He warned both Charlie and Blackie that if they started anything he'd send them off.

The game was only five minutes old when Charlie Onions took his cap off to Blackie. Immediately the referee intervened and warned both of them that the next time it happened they would be sent off.

Five minutes later and Charlie again had his cap off to Blackie after a tackle that nearly parted him from his ankles.

The referee raced up to them.

'Off, off,' he shouted. The two players looked at one another.

'Nay, ref, we're only just warmin' up,' said Charlie.

'Off, off,' said the ref, who was getting very excited.

Blackie said, 'Na' look, ref, me and Charlie don't

mean 'owt when we start fightin' and it's what t'crowd expects. So why don't tha' leave us alone?'

The ref was nearly beside himself with frustration and rage. 'Off, off or else I abandon the game,' he shouted.

Blackie looked at Charlie Onions and said, 'Tha' knows, Charlie, I've played this game fifteen years and nivver been sent off, and I've allus said when I do get t'marching orders it will be for summat special. Na', old mate, I don't regard cloggin' thee as being owt special, does tha'?' Charlie shook his head. 'Therefore,' said Blackie, 'I'm about to mek a proper job of things.' Whereupon he turned to the referee and felled him with a colossal right swing.

Two weeks later Blackie was in the boozer when they brought the news. Len, the trainer, said to him, 'They've banned thi' *sine die*.'

'Is that bad?' asked Blackie.

'It means for good, that's all,' said Len.

'That's all right then. I wor ready for retirin', any road,' said Blackie.

Blackie didn't suffer. Later that season they held a benefit game for him. The posters advertising the game said 'Proceeds for a deserving charity' because they couldn't announce they were collecting for a banned player. The referee, on the other hand, got little sympathy from anyone, and eventually went to live in Wakefield.

If you go back to the village now they'll still point Blackie out to you, and tell you how he fixed the referee.

All he did was to express in one massive right-arm

swing what anyone who has ever been to a football match has felt at one time or another. We've all nurtured a secret desire to chin the referee. Knowing this, and knowing also that the referee is aware of it too, I am filled with wonderment and amazement every time I see them trot on to the field of play. How many men do you know who would walk into the jaws of hell knowing that their only reward is a few bob and the scorn of their fellow men?

THE TALLER THEY ARE . . .

SERIOUS-MINDED students of soccer such as myself are finding it increasingly difficult to chart the course of the modern game. No sooner do we master the new tactical innovations, such as everyone wearing everyone else's shirt, than we find ourselves face to face with some new subtlety.

The most recent development in the game was heralded by Tony Hateley and Wyn Davies, two tall centre-forwards, being transferred for very large sums of money. Justifying their outlay, the managers of the clubs that bought them gave a hint to soccer's next phase.

Both managers declared their firm belief that football matches in the future are going to be won in the air. They have decided that the only way to beat packed defences is to sling high crosses on to the hard head of a very tall centre-forward in the hope that he will nod the ball into goal.

The simplicity of the idea is appealing, and a welcome sign that after all the technical clap-trap being talked about soccer recently some people at least have come around to the idea that it is a simple game, watched by simple people.

This latest development is, of course, of great significance to very tall centre-forwards who don't mind what they do with their heads. A new life of glamour and riches is theirs for the taking.

The problem here is one of genetics. We are not a very tall people. I read somewhere that the average Englishman is 5ft 9ins, reads the *Daily Express* and has two pairs of false teeth in his lifetime. So one can see that if the latest development in soccer is to come to pass, football managers will have to look elsewhere for their material.

This is where tall people, like the Tutsi of Rwanda and Burundi and Ona of Tierra del Fuego, Chile, come into their own. The giant men of these tribes should stop whatever they are doing and start learning to head a football.

Scene: An encampment of the Tutsi, a proud and tall warrior race. Sixteen football managers from England sit in an improvised stand, their pockets stuffed with cheap trinkets and book tokens. On a rough-and-ready patch hacked out of the bush, Tutsi Albion are playing Tutsi Dynamo (using turbans for goalposts). The centre of attraction is Lionel N'gooda, the dynamic centre-forward of Tutsi Albion.

Lionel stands 8ft 9ins in his cheap plastic football boots made in Hong Kong. He scores twelve goals in the game, all with his head, and afterwards is surrounded by football managers fighting for his services. Eventually he is sold to Chelsea for eight tubes of wine gums, two cases of cheap Australian sherry and three plastic raincoats.

In England Lionel is an immediate success. Desmond Dribbel calls him 'Leaping Lionel,' and says of him, 'N'gooda is V'gooda. A black panther, a dusky sensation.'

Lionel scores seventy-two goals in his first season with Chelsea, all with his head. Soon he opens his first boutique called, 'I'm High Daddy. Clothes for the taller man.' He is frequently seen in the company of Tommy Docherty. The canny Scot says, 'Lionel speaks very good English.' He is even more frequently seen with Lady Daphne Kippington-Bedsprings, London's tallest deb, who says, 'I always felt out of it until I met Lionel.'

Like all successful people, Lionel makes enemies. A group of soccer managers, meeting secretly, decide that the only way to combat this growing menace of tall centre-forwards is to find even taller centre-halves. They employ the brilliant but evil talents of Professor J. Achestein-Fink.

In his laboratory in Zürich the Professor, the man who developed the jumbo drug for shot-putters and the 'anything-you-can-do' pill for women hammer-throwers, works on a new invention to beat the menace of Leaping Lionel.

After six months he develops a drug to stretch the legs and harden the head. He experiments on a 5ft 6ins centre-half who once played for Chesterfield. The experiment is completely successful. The centre-half grows to 9ft 2ins, can head guided missiles and is transferred to Tottenham Hotspur for £120,000.

In his first game against Lionel he so dominates him that the Tutsi pulls a knife and is sent from the field. Soon every First Division club in England has one of Professor Achestein-Fink's centre-halves, and the

Professor is able to buy Noël Coward's house in Bermuda and retire.

Lionel is unable to score any more goals and Tommy Docherty twice sends him back to his digs because he has not cleaned his teeth. Lionel eventually sells his boutique and returns to his native village where he finds his relatives have eaten his transfer fee.

In the meantime Bob Lord, Britain's caped crusader, protests to FIFA about what he calls 'these disgusting trends in our great national game'. Mr Lord bans from his ground any player standing more than 6ft 3ins, saying, 'It's not natural.'

The Minister for Sport intervenes and makes a plea for 'normalcy'. Swift action follows. The FA bans from the game any man standing more than 6ft 3ins. Bob Lord says, 'It's a triumph for northern common sense.' The eighteen giant centre-halves in the First Division are given free transfers and are hired by an American football promoter to play exhibition matches against a team of Pygmies.

Desmond Dribbel sums up. In a no-punches-pulled editorial headed 'This Sorry Mess' he concludes, 'It proves what I said at the beginning of this sad and sorry affair: the taller they are, the harder they fall.'

Skull skill

F UNNY HOW the trapdoor of my memory is sprung by incidents of the moment. Only the other day I was minding my own business, taking a stroll, when I happened on a game of soccer. Two local teams were hard at it, boring the pants off the three spectators and each other, when there occurred something that reached into the back pocket of my mind.

One of the teams gained a free kick just outside the penalty area and it was taken by a player built like a butcher's dog and wearing the demeanour of the village hangman. He raced thirty yards and toe-ended the ball, heavy as a suet pudding, at the wall of defenders. The velocity of the shot was sufficient to cause the wall to break and scatter, all except for one player who not only remained at his post but flung himself headlong at the missile.

When the top of his head hit the ball the impact must have been similar to two inter-city trains colliding head-on. Surprisingly though, the defender with the kamikaze tendencies survived, nay, more than that, he prospered. The ball hurtled from his head way over the halfway line and the centre-forward, who was enjoying a break while picking his nose, nipped through to score.

'He does it regular,' said the local standing next to me. 'Can't play football but he can't half head a ball.'

I was back in time twenty years or so and standing on the terraces at Barnsley watching a centre-half called Archie Whyte, who would head cannon balls. He had the broadest brow of anyone I've ever seen, including Beethoven, and it was pock-marked and hillocked with the scars of his craft.

He was something, but the best of them all was 'Muscle' Eadie. He was a large, friendly youth with a large unfriendly mother who prepared her son for life's highways and byways by regularly thumping him on the head with a small coal shovel. Having survived a dozen or more years of this treatment he developed an immunity to blows on his skull, and on the football field gained a considerable reputation as a header of the ball.

Although he played centre-half for our team his speciality was saving penalty kicks. Whenever we had one awarded against us, which was just about every game, Muscle would send the goalie away and stand on the goalline.

'What's tha' up to?' the ref would say. 'I'm going to save this penalty,' said Muscle. 'How's tha' going to do that? Tha' can't use thi' hands tha' knows,' said the

referee. 'I know that, ref. I'm going to stop it wi' mi' 'ead,' said Muscle.

This would always prove too much for the penalty taker who, instead of keeping cool and placing the ball, would feel challenged to knock Muscle's head from his shoulders. Many tried but none succeeded. The inevitable result of aiming at a spot just between Muscle's eyes was that the ball ended up fifty yards behind the penalty taker.

Off the field he made a handsome living heading anything for money. For instance, whenever the fair came to the village we'd all turn up at the coconut shy to win one for Muscle. Armed with our coconut he'd throw it high in the air and then head it. This act inevitably drew a large crowd and very soon we'd be going round the punters laying odds that Muscle could head the coconut three times running, and more than that, break it.

He never failed and was so good at it that the man who ran the coconut shy made a serious offer for Muscle to tour with him. All he had to do was stand in for the coconuts and let people throw things at his head, but he declined, saying he had better things to do. It was on the football field that he put his marvellous skull to the most effective use. He used his forehead not simply as a defensive weapon but often in an offensive role.

He was virtually unstoppable from dead-ball situations, launching himself at the ball like a guided missile, scattering opponents and heading goals from the most unlikely positions.

I'd not seen Muscle for ages, and then I went back

home to visit an old friend. We'd had a night out supping a few and were walking back to our house when we saw a figure lying on the pavement. It was Muscle, drunk as a monkey. We picked him up and took him home. At least I took him to the house where he used to live when we were kids. The back door was open and we dumped him in the kitchen.

My friend who had led a life more sheltered than mine had not met Muscle before.

'Who is he?' he asked as we walked the damp streets home.

'He's an old mate. His name's Muscle Eadie,' I said.

'What's his claim to fame?' my friend asked.

'You're not going to believe this, but he heads coconuts,' I said.

'You've been away too long,' said my friend.

CODY'S CONGS

I SUPPOSE that when they come to write the history of football, one of the most significant events of the present era will be seen to be the emergence of the manager out of the shadows and into the spotlight. In the murky past, though, there were always exceptions; the manager was the man who paid the wages, made sure the balls were blown up and weeded the terracing. It was not a glamorous job and, in the main, it begat anonymity, although there was one manager who achieved both fame and glamour, albeit in an unusual way.

He became enamoured of the tea lady at the club, and they spent many magic moments together when he should have been weeding the terracing, and she should have been making the tea.

The scene of their romantic interludes was the directors' toilet, it being the perfect secret meeting place for lovers because it was uninhabited except on matchdays. One day the passionate couple managed to lock themselves in, and had to be rescued by the fire brigade. No one believed the manager's excuse that he was looking for his cufflinks, and that the tea lady had been helping him. The matter was discreetly reported in the local paper, and there were an extra 2,000 at the next home game hoping to catch a glimpse of the tea lady.

Little did we know at the time that there would come

a day when managers like Clough and Allison would pull in the crowds without having to indulge in such bizarre escapades. Mind you, it's my view that managers have always been slightly potty. We notice them more nowadays because what happens on the field is infinitely less interesting than that which happens in the manager's office.

The best manager I ever played for bossed a team called Cody's Congs. He was manager and a one-man board of directors because he owned the field, the footballs, the nets and the lorry that took us to away games.

He also owned the shirts that gave us our name. What happened was that he had a brother-in-law who worked for Cody's Circus which went bust. Our manager bought a lot of the bankrupt stock, including a dozen T-shirts which differed from ordinary football shirts only in that they had names and not numbers on the backs. Thus I became the only centre-forward that I know of to play a season with Ramon The Dwarf on my back.

The tactical advantages of our strip were enormous. Not many defenders looking for our right-winger tumbled he was Carlos the Fire Eater, or that our inside-right was the man with Sheba and Her Pythons on his back. We took full advantage of their bewilderment and went through a season undefeated. Sadly for us and the cause of brighter football, we were ordered by the league's management committee to wear traditional shirts for the coming season.

This precipitated a financial crisis in the club, which

16/07/2002 14:43   A00002   T02-082092
£

0000001264928 SLEEVE DETAIL C	25.00
0000001316900 THROW LS JAPANE	12.50
0000001333947 ST GEORGE SS PR	10.00

Total To Pay   £47.50

SWITCH Tendered   £47.50
491182450500305816
Expiry Date : 01/03
Issue Number: 2
Swiped

Merchant Id : 11479661

Cardholder - Please retain for
your records

Cardholder's copy

Change   £0.00

Refund Policy-
USC will be pleased to exchange
any item returned to us, provided
it is in its original condition and
accompanied by proof of purchase.
Cash refunds will only be given
if the item purchased does not
comply with the requirements
of the Sale of Goods Act 1979
(as amended). This does not
affect your statutory rights.

**USC is a division of USC Group Plc
Registered office: 4 Maxwell Square,
Brucefield Business Park,
Livingston, EH54 9BL.**

Refund Policy-
USC will be pleased to exchange
any item returned to us, provided
it is in its original condition and
accompanied by proof of purchase.
Cash refunds will only be given
if the item purchased does not
comply with the requirements
of the Sale of Goods Act 1979
(as amended). This does not
affect your statutory rights.

**USC is a division of USC Group Plc
Registered office: 4 Maxwell Square,
Brucefield Business Park,
Livingston, EH54 9BL.**

Refund Policy-
USC will be pleased to exchange

was solved by Elsie, our manager's wife. During the summer she knitted an entire set of football shirts. So it came to be that we took the field for the opening game of the season attired in shirts of double-strength fisherman's yarn which would have been useful for arctic explorers but were entirely unsuitable for ninety minutes non-stop action on a soccer pitch. We only wore them once because the first time Elsie washed them they shrunk, so we were back to the Cody's Circus shirts, which we wore inside out to hide the name tags.

Elsie was a great one with the knitting needles. She once knitted a pullover for a chicken in our team colours. Our manager kept chickens, and one day after selecting a bird for the pot and wringing its neck, was halfway through plucking it when the unfortunate bird revived. Our manager didn't have the heart to finish the job off, so he settled for a bird with a sore neck and minus half its feathers. It became our mascot and the ever-practical Elsie knitted it a little jumper to keep it warm.

Sadly, the wretched creature didn't last long because one of our manager's neighbours with a cruel sense of humour complained that the bird was upsetting his wife,

who had seen it leaving the outside toilet buttoning its flies. Whereas the rest of us appreciated the joke, our manager and Elsie took it seriously, and our mascot ended up on the dinner table with a pound of sage and onion stuffed inside it.

Elsie was the mother figure to our football team. She washed the kit, made the tea, patched our wounds, darned our socks and for a time, became the only woman trainer in the whole of football. This experiment lasted only until Big Clacker, our centre-half, got kicked in the unmentionables and was altogether too precise in his language when Elsie arrived on the scene and asked him what had happened.

Her only other venture on to the field of play was during a particularly dirty game against a local pit team, when the opposing centre-forward put our goalkeeper and the ball in the back of the net. Herbert, our goalkeeper, belonged to Elsie. I say belonged, because although he called her Mam, he wasn't her son. Rumour was that Elsie had a sister in Barnsley who had an affair with an Italian prisoner of war and Herbert was the issue of that unlikely liaison. However, no Mum could have loved a son as passionately as Elsie loved Herbert.

The sight of him lying bloodied in the back of the net was too much. As the centre-forward turned to embrace his colleagues, he was confronted by Elsie, who bashed him with her handbag. She would have done worse, had she not been grabbed by the referee.

Thereafter she stayed at home, which proved a wise decision, because during the return game the centre-

forward she had assaulted brought along his mother,
who looked a bit like Sydney Greenstreet, except she
weighed more.

'What happened to thi mother?' asked the centre-
forward. 'Got knocked down by a bus,' lied Herbert.

'That's nowt to what's going to happen to thee,' said
the centre-forward. And he was as good as his word.

Among her many talents, Elsie was a soothsayer.
Every Saturday morning at the team gathering she would
empty the cups and read the tea leaves. Our right-
winger, Charlie Donkin, wouldn't play if the message
wasn't favourable.

'You will meet a big black man today,' Elsie would
say, peering at the tea leaves.

'Blackies don't play football,' said Charlie.

'He's in his pit muck,' Elsie explained.

'Owt else?' asked Charlie.

'A white man and a man in a white coat,' said Elsie.

'Christ, an ambulance,' said Charlie. 'I'm going to get
a leg broke.'

'Load of nonsense,' said our manager.

But it made no difference. Charlie went home and
stayed in bed, only getting up at opening time to go to
the boozer, whereupon he was knocked down by an
ice-cream van driven by a man wearing a white overall.
He didn't break his leg, but it cured him of Elsie.

I digress only to underline the problem facing the
manager of a football team, whether it be Cody's Congs
or Leeds United. Our manager stuck with Cody's Congs
for about four seasons until he discovered the joys of

women's football. He organised a team from the local stocking factory, and ended up leaving Elsie and her knitting needles to live in sin with his centre-half, a strapping lass with legs like Bobby Charlton.

Now all that happened a long time ago, but surely the peccadilloes of our present race of football managers only go to show that nothing has changed. Managers of football teams are the odd bods of our society. The axiom that you have to have a slate loose to be a football manager is as true today as it ever was. I'm not saying you have to be barmy to manage a football team, but it certainly helps.

Backstreet goalies who stood head and shoulders below the rest

THE DEBATE in soccer about moving the goalposts is nothing new. It was already a fully fledged issue when I started playing backstreet soccer nearly fifty years ago.

In those days the rules stated that the goals should be as wide as the size of the goalkeeper times three. This required the goalie to lie down while we placed a coat at his feet and repeat the process twice more whereupon we put the other coat at his head. This meant there were not many tall goalkeepers to be found in our league. They all tended to be on the dwarfish side of small.

Size was also important in judging where the crossbar was. Crossbars were owned only by proper football clubs so we had to make an agreed assessment of where it might be in relation to the goalkeeper's height. The arguments over whether the shot would have hit the crossbar, cleared it or even hit the underside and bounced down over the line, sometimes verged on the metaphysical but invariably ended in violence and tears. We solved the problem by learning to keep the ball low when shooting.

My father told me that he once saw Steve Bloomer,

a prolific goalscorer for Derby County and Middles-brough, take a penalty against 'Fatty' Foulke, the Sheffield United goalkeeper, who was a huge man weighing about 20 stone. It was a wet and soggy day at Bramall Lane when the ball was like a lead shot. Bloomer, renowned for his strength, struck the ball straight at Foulke's midriff whereupon, having caught the ball, the goalkeeper was propelled over the goalline into the back of the net like a man skiing backwards. My old man reckoned Steve Bloomer was doing it for a bet, but I knew that it was the supreme example of a tactic learned during an apprenticeship in backyard soccer.

The only time we had a proper framework for a goal was when we dared to play against the garage door at the top of our street. Not unnaturally, the man who owned it objected to his freshly painted door being used as a target by muddy footballs, so games had a tendency to be interrupted. But the joy of seeing the imprint of your match-winning shot on the green woodwork remains with me to this day.

Indeed, when I rose to head Sippy Salt's cross into the top right-hand corner to beat Gonk Reynolds's team by the odd goal of thirty-three, it was the proudest moment of my life. It didn't matter that my run towards the Royal Box was interrupted by the garage owner who prevented me receiving the Cup from the King by chasing me across two fields and threatening to send for PC Williams. PC Williams was feared by every youngster who visited Barnsley FC in those days. And a lot of us did.

Just after the war, 20,000 spectators at Oakwell was an average gate. PC Williams would stroll around the field before the game to demonstrate his presence. On the odd occasion when there was a disturbance in the crowd, he would beckon with his forefinger at the offender who would often voluntarily give himself up and be escorted around the ground and out of it by the constable.

The only time the matter might be taken further was if the culprit failed to obey the beckoning finger. This would necessitate PC Williams making – for him – two extravagant and unnecessary gestures, namely laying his cape on the turf and then hopping over the wall into the crowd. When this happened you could be sure that the offender would not be seen for a month or two at home matches, having been warned off by the good constable. FIFA should find PC Williams and seek his views on security at the next World Cup.

Thinking of Sippy Salt reminded me of another important contribution that backyard soccer leagues made to more entertaining soccer – the closet winger. These were the wingmen who employed their skills by flicking the ball against the closet wall, racing past the

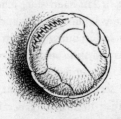

opponent, and taking the return pass off the brickwork. Stanley Matthews was a closet winger, so was Tom Finney; Johnny Kelly, at Barnsley, was another.

By the way, having written about the way Kelly shaped the future of English soccer by giving Alf Ramsey a terrible time when Southampton came to Barnsley, thereby creating Sir h'Alf's hatred of wingers, I had a letter from a historian of the game asking if I could give a date for this momentous event. It was 2 October 1948, and the Barnsley team was Pat Kelly, Williams, Pallister, Normanton, Whyte, Glover, Smith, Griffiths, Robledo, Baxter and Johnny Kelly. I also recall Southampton had a goalkeeper called Black, that Ramsey was right full-back, that Ted Bates played inside-forward, Charlie Wayman was centre-forward and that they had a left-winger called Gallego. I only remember his name because my mate, Quinn, who was a bit of a swot, wondered if he was related to the man who perfected the refracting telescope. I said I didn't know but thought it highly unlikely. Quinn went to Cambridge so he probably found out before I did.

Anyway, my mate Sippy Salt was close-on the best closet winger I played with. It didn't matter if the closets were on his right or left-hand side, made of wood or brick. On song he was unstoppable and when I broke the goalscoring record of our street team with 163 goals in a season (the record still stands, unlike the closets) it was mainly due to the service provided by him.

If we are to be serious for a moment, the decline of the winger in British football is generally accepted as

having commenced with the appointment of Sir h'Alf as England's team manager in the sixties. I think it started earlier than that with the introduction of inside toilets into houses in the north of England. The demolition of the outside closet was the death of the old-fashioned dribbler. It is well worth FIFA looking closely at this subject as they deliberate ways and means of making soccer in the future more attractive. It is, after all, only by looking at our history that we discover the future.

That being the case, let me offer one or two recollections of the past that might be of help to today's hard-pressed administrators. They must not believe that the problems they are facing in the modern game are either new or insurmountable. Indeed they are almost piffling compared to some of the problems we had to sort out in the Barnsley and District Backyard League. Our league was dominated for several seasons by a side skippered by a psychopath who wore a cloth cap that he would often remove to chastise his opponents with a good nebbing. (To neb: old Yorkshire pastime; to beat about the head with the furled peak of a cap.) He neutered our closet wingers by removing the doors to the outside toilet on matchdays. But his most successful tactic was the use of his pet dog. This creature looked like a cross between a collie and an alligator and would bite anyone who came within five yards of its owner. If the side happened to be a couple of goals down, a whistle would bring the dog on to the field whereupon its master would, unchallenged, score the goals required for victory. We had to wait until the dog ran under a coal lorry before things changed. I offer that anecdote to FIFA only to show that if they think they've got problems they don't know they're born.

However, a practical suggestion for speeding up play concerns the way that modern players spend an inordinate amount of time rolling around in agony over some alleged foul when they ought to be on their feet running after a football, which is what they are paid for in the first place. This is always a problem area for referees because assessing if the player is genuinely hurt or simply shamming is difficult.

A team I played for once solved this problem by employing a trainer whose infallible method of discovering if a player was really injured or not was to begin his examination by biting him on the neck. The sight of him running on to the field, fitting his false teeth as he approached, was enough to deter any malingerer. Indeed, I have seen men with shattered limbs attempt to struggle to their feet to escape his diagnosis. One of the problems about being bitten by him was you didn't know whose teeth he was wearing at the time. He would make a random selection from his sponge bag, which was where he stored his players' teeth for safekeeping. Again I am not suggesting that modern trainers go around biting their players but I do think there is enough evidence of its effectiveness as an antidote to a problem still with us to warrant further investigation by FIFA.

I hope they take my suggestions seriously in Zurich.

They might sound barmy but the people at FIFA are used to that. It was they, after all, who gave the next World Cup to the Yanks.

December 1990

BARNSLEY AND SKINNER

LOOKING BACK TO
SCHOOLDAYS, I ONLY
CARE TO REMEMBER
WHAT HAPPENED ON THE
PLAYING FIELDS

I was talking to a chap the other day who was going on about the state of sport in our schools. He was making the point that at present the education system was doing for British sport what Dutch Elm disease did for our landscape. In some instances, even if teachers wanted to teach a sport they couldn't because the playing fields have been sold off. I started thinking if that had happened at my school I wouldn't have bothered turning up. I learned two skills at Barnsley Grammar School – how to smoke and how to play cricket. Both have proved lifelong afflictions.

In those days, before the educational theorists got to work, competitive sport was an important part of the curriculum. It would have been easier for the headmaster to fire the Latin master than to get rid of our sports teacher. I regarded academic subjects as being what we did in between the periods set aside for games. So did many of my friends, and, I suspect, one or two of our teachers.

Mr Swift, who taught cricket, soccer and maths, was

renowned for gazing longingly towards the cricket field while teaching algebra on a summer's day. He could be easily deflected from a lecture on geometry by the proposition that if Pythagoras was alive and playing for Yorkshire he would bowl seam up like Mr Coxon, not leg breaks and chinamen like Mr Wardle. Looking back to my schooldays, I care to remember only what happened on the playing fields. The rest was a waste of time. I spent a while trying to remember what I did at school when I wasn't being taught cricket by Webb Swift and the answer was being taught soccer by Webb Swift.

He had been a semi-pro with Halifax, I think – but whereas his love of cricket was based on its subtle and profound mysteries, his relationship with soccer was much more direct. As a centre-half, 'get stuck in' and 'get rid' was about as deep as he intended to go when asked to elaborate his theory. He had no time for 'fancy' players and would reward their ambitions with a swift kicking. He was, of course, in the great tradition of Barnsley defenders like Skinner Normanton (whom God preserve) and epitomised by the great pre-war trio of Harper, Henderson and Holley. Old Tom Holley became a journalist when he stopped kicking people for

Barnsley and Leeds, and I used to sit next to him in the press box where he would upbraid me for extolling the virtues of the great Skinner.

'He were soft compared to them at Barnsley when I played theer,' said Tom. Then he'd get all misty eyed as he remembered the havoc he'd caused. 'Ay, 'arper, 'enderson and 'olley. Not much escaped our clutches, I can tell you,' he said.

It might have been Tom, or if it wasn't it was someone else who wore the No. 5 shirt at Barnsley, who would greet the opposing No. 9 with the words, 'Before we start tha's got a choice, Barnsley Beckett Hospital or Sheffield Royal Infirmary.'

Barnsley crowds appreciated raw meat. As children they were reared on it through contact with teachers like Webb Swift. Whereas I won his approval by my dogged approach to batting, I also incurred his wrath by my delicate manner on a soccer field. I never cared for the crunch of physical battle and I think Mr Swift had me down as a bit of a nancy. It was therefore as a spectator and not a participant that I watched a Masters versus Boys match which featured a clash between Mr Swift and a young man called Duncan Sharpe.

Duncan didn't need any coaching from Webb Swift. When he arrived at Barnsley Grammar School he was a fully fledged assassin of ball-playing forwards. They went for a fifty-fifty ball and with a terrible clash of studs and bone, burst through the ring of watching spectators and slid down the bank on to the school play-ground. When they stood up they both looked like they had been involved in a bad road accident, but the two of them were laughing. I knew then that Duncan Sharpe would play for Barnsley. And he did. During the time he wore the No. 5 shirt it was said that certain centre-forwards of nervous disposition were known to take sick with a mysterious illness a couple of days before they faced Duncan Sharpe at Oakwell.

You could argue that my education was a touch lop-sided. But no more so than those children who for one reason or another are nowadays denied a playing field or a sports master. At least in my day we had a choice. What is sad about today's set-up is that it has no place for the Webb Swifts of teaching. Where they flourish still is where they always have and always will, at public schools. Down the road in the state system, the discrepancy between those who pay for their children and those who don't becomes more and more apparent. It's not fair and it doesn't make sense. We should seek out our politicians and tell them so, but we won't. We've always had a non-chalant attitude towards sport, which is why our schools are in the state they are. Every Wimbledon we bellyache about our tennis players without doing anything about a system that would require a miracle to produce a winner.

I have never doubted the importance of sport in the education of the child. As I sit here writing this article, I am reminded that although judged by academic standards my five years at Barnsley Grammar School were a complete waste of time, what I did learn there has enabled me to earn a living while pretending to be working. In other words the job is the hobby and the hobby the job. I can't think of a better preparation for life than that. Can you?

June 1990

Mine closures sound death knell of great sporting tradition

G AVIN SMITH died in 1992. He was seventy-three and had been retired from his job as a hospital porter for nearly ten years. Before that he was the licensee of a pub and before that, in his golden youth, he ran like the wind down the right wing for Barnsley.

He was so swift he needed an arresting parachute to prevent him colliding with the crowd. He was the one they built the gate in the wall for so that he could continue his fastest gallops through the terraces and out of the ground before pulling up in the car park.

He loved cutting inside and scoring goals. They were always spectacular, often causing the *Green 'Un* to report: 'Smith's explosive shot bulged the net behind the hapless custodian.' He was much helped by a young Irishman called Danny Blanchflower whose ability to pass behind defenders gave vivid challenge to Smith's acceleration.

As if this wasn't enough of a feast, on the other wing was Johnny Kelly, who dawdled, tricked and conned his way through defences. He was a pickpocket of a player, Smith a battering ram. One of his greatest moments came in the 1945–46 season when Barnsley played Newcastle United in the FA Cup. In the first leg, in front of 60,000 at Newcastle, Barnsley lost 4–2. The return leg was played at Barnsley the following Wednesday and I stood with my father in the rain along with 27,000 other supporters for our first view of players like Ernie Taylor, Joe Harvey, Albert Stubbins and Jackie Milburn. The interest in the game was such that the local pits had sanctioned a day off with a notice which read: 'In order that the management may have knowledge of the number intending to be absent on Wednesday afternoon, will those whose relatives are to be buried on that day please apply by Tuesday for permission to attend.'

We won 3–0 and not too many went down the pit the next day either. Gavin Smith scored the second goal, racing through the defence, cutting in and smashing the ball past King. It was poignant recalling that day of noisy crowds and silent pits at a time when politicians have decided we no longer need a coal industry.

When I was growing up the link between club and mine was irrevocable. Not only did the pit provide the spectators, it also employed the players. They shared a common experience with the people who came to watch them on a Saturday afternoon. The relationship was

deep and complete. It defined the character of clubs like Barnsley. The ground told you what to expect. As you breasted the hill from the bus station it sat there guarded by slag heaps. The streets of weatherbeaten stone houses came right down to the main gate.

The pits also provided a certain kind of player. He was likely to be of medium height and sturdy build, and uncompromising in a tackle. In my time at Barnsley, the wonderful Skinner Normanton epitomised the breed, but there were others. In fact, they were in unending supply. All you had to do was to peer down any pit shaft and whistle and one came up, ready to go to work.

Things have changed; soccer has become homogenised. When Allan Clarke was player-manager at Barnsley, I went to see them play at Reading. We lost 7–0. It was one of the saddest days of my life and Mr Clarke wasn't too chuffed either. The worst insult came with Reading six goals up when a Barnsley fan shouted to a perplexed Clarke, 'Why doesn't tha' put Parky on?'

I was not surprised to read that the next week Mr Clarke took his players down the local pit to remind them what hard graft was really like. We mourn the disappearance of a sporting tradition that enriched the lives of those lucky enough to experience it. It is possible to glamorise the realities of life in a mining community, but it is not possible to invent the humour, drama, colour and enchantment provided by soccer teams like Barnsley in the days when they were suckled by the community they served. In future years when my grandchildren visit their ancestral home, there will be little

left of what I have described. The slag heaps will be landscaped, the stadium an all-seater and the car park where Gavin Smith used to finish his runs will be a hotel and leisure centre.

Smith and Blanchflower, Kelly and Baxter, Skinner and Tommy Taylor, Cec McCormack and Gordon Pallister will be ghostly figures in a forgotten landscape. My grandchildren will be told that it was ugly and grimy in those days. I want them to know that it wasn't pretty, but we made the best of it and, on looking back, it had a terrible grandeur.

October 1992

THERE'S NOWT TO BRAG
ABOUT FOR BARNSLEY

T HE LAST TIME Barnsley won the FA Cup, Captain
Scott reached Antarctica, Kaiser Bill was fifty-two
and the *Titanic* hit an iceberg. They used to fly a pennant
over the main stand bearing the message 'Barnsley: FA
Cup Winners 1912'. Part of the initiation ceremony for
a place on the terraces at Oakwell was to name the
eleven who brought the Cup to Barnsley: Cooper;
Downs, Taylor; Glendenning, Bratley, Utley; Bartrop,
Tufnell, Lillycrop, Travers and Moore.

To support Barnsley it helped if you had a good
memory, and a long one. On Saturday, walking round
the pleasant Bromsgrove ground before the FA Cup
third-round tie, I was stopped by an old man who
wanted to know if I ever met George Lillycrop. I said I
didn't have the good fortune to watch Barnsley the last
time they won the Cup. 'Just wondered,' he said. It was
a curious introduction for a very strange day.

For one thing, Bromsgrove does not feel like a football
town. It is far too sedate to accommodate comfortably
the hostile challenge associated with an FA Cup tie, too
polite to do anything other than shrug off the raucous
confrontation on offer from visiting fans who treat every
trip outside their own backyard as an expedition
through an alien landscape.

Some Barnsley fans I talked to were surprised to find

the pubs open, although one establishment had put up a sign: 'We Only Serve Regulars'. Outside the busiest pub in town, a plain-clothes policeman was using a video camera to record the comings and goings. As I watched the operation, I was approached by a woman who asked if we were filming a 'This is Your Life' programme.

The *Bromsgrove Messenger* said that the visit of Barnsley was the biggest day in the history of the club and reported 'Bubbly Rovers Set Sights On Victory'. It seemed an unduly over-optimistic assessment of what might happen, particularly when you studied the pen portraits of the two teams and compared Barnsley's team of full-time professionals with Bromsgrove's part-timers. They included a window fitter, an accountant, three players who are currently unemployed and another who will not play soccer on a Saturday because it is against his religion. Yet the wonder of the FA Cup is that it gives the underdogs the chance to defy logic and bring a whiff of romance to a game which, in the normal course of events, has little time for such soppy stuff.

Barnsley had an early indication that they were in for a bumpy ride when Recky Carter, a contender for the Tony Daley Award for the Worst Haircut in Soccer, galloped through an admiring Barnsley defence to hit goalkeeper Butler when it would have been easier to put the ball in the net.

It was Carter who slid the ball through a Barnsley defence as rigid as a parade of guardsmen for Crisp to score and set the home crowd gibbering with delight.

With Barnsley's right flank under pressure, things were no better on the left-hand side of the park. There a young toothpick called Colin Radburn galloped passed defenders with the kind of insouciant disregard for reputation that would have brought terrible retribution from one or two Barnsley defenders I used to watch.

To say Barnsley played badly would be understating the case. They did not play at all until it was almost too late. In the first half, they were almost embarrassingly incompetent. In the second half, they at least tried to suggest the difference between the two teams by attempting to play skilful football.

Even then, there was nothing to suggest they were playing a team three divisions below them. Richardson, at the heart of the Bromsgrove defence, had a wonderful, robust game. He is the sort of defender who careers around the field and clatters into people. It sounds random, but on Saturday his tackling had the accuracy of a heat-seeking missile. He once stopped Archdeacon with a noise like a car crash; but the Barnsley player recovered to take terrible revenge. First, he floated the ball in from a corner for Rammell to loop in a soft and undeserved equaliser. Then he won the game, striking a sweet left-foot shot from Liddell's intelligent pass.

Sport can be cruel and deceitful. It can make monkeys out of sane men. Before Barnsley scored, even the mature supporters of the home team were hugging each other, giving the thumbs up, chanting 'Away, Away Bromsgrove', looking forward to beating Manchester United in the next round. The next minute, they were desolate and bereft, choked with despair. A couple of hundred Barnsley fans invaded the pitch but, in truth, they had little to celebrate. The man on the loudspeaker pleaded with the Bromsgrove fans not to become involved in confrontation. 'Show them we are better than they are,' he exhorted. Their team already had.

January 1994

GROWING UP ON
THE TERRACES

I FIRST PLANTED my feet on the terraces at Barnsley when I was five and I spent the next fifteen years or more rooted to the spot. My position changed according to my rate of growth. For the first few years I rested my chin on the concrete wall separating the players from the spectators and saw many wondrous things.

We had a centre-half called Kitchen who specialised in sliding tackles designed to take the winger and the ball into touch. They were spectacular efforts, often launched some distance from the target who would be dillying and dallying with his foot on the ball when, suddenly and without warning, he would end up in a twisted heap at the bottom of our wall amid a terrible noise of stud on bone.

Kitchen rarely missed. He was like a heat-seeking missile. Once locked on to his subject they were doomed. There were those who swore that Kitchen had so perfected his technique that midway through his sliding tackle he could swerve round obstacles, like team-mates who got in his way.

I can't confirm that but I do remember the one occasion when he missed his target. The winger jumped at the last minute and Kitchen slid underneath him like a runaway bull and hit the concrete wall full on. The damage was considerable, with concrete chips flying in all directions. The result was so spectacular that those of us in the frontline who were showered with debris turned up at future games wearing motorbike goggles to protect our eyes and to honour our hero.

What visiting wingers who had to patrol our touchline made of us I don't know – not that they expected anything other than a hard time when they visited Barnsley. The chorus from the terraces whenever a member of the opposition was hit in the unmentionables and was being approached by the trainer with magic sponge and mopping bucket, was, 'Nay lad, don't wash 'em. Count 'em.'

In those days, trainers looked like window cleaners and the likelihood was that when they weren't looking after players on a Saturday afternoon, they might well shine windows for a living. Similarly, the winger who cheered so lustily on Saturday afternoon might well be working alongside you down the pit on Monday morning.

If you waited long enough after a game at Oakwell, you could travel home on the same bus as your hero. In those days there was a proximity between fans and players, a relationship betwixt the community and the club. All that changed, as inevitably it had to, but it was lovely and warm and fulfilling while it lasted. Those were the days before the songs of support and the concerted chanting. This was the time when the lone and often despairing voice of dissent was heard from the terraces. Brentford were playing at Barnsley one day and had in their ranks a full-back called Gorman. He was a good player but bald as a coot. It was a sunny day and Gorman's head was glistening in the sun. He went to head the ball and it slid from his pate for a throw-in. 'Tha' wants to put some bloody chalk on it, Gorman,' said a man standing near to us.

Those were the days when fans of both teams were allowed to stand together and there was intelligent competition for the observations of the day. The standard was high and excluded foul language.

My all-time favourite remark was made by a visiting Chesterfield supporter who watched silently as his team prepared to take a penalty in the dying seconds of a game at Barnsley, which would have given them the draw. Games between Chesterfield and Barnsley were always keenly fought when Chesterfield had defenders like Ray Middleton in goal, Kidd and Milburn, as formidable and frightening a pair of full-backs as ever kicked a winger, and forwards of the quality and class of Linacre and Capel.

Capel was the captain on this day and he ordered up his brother to take the important penalty kick. The unfortunate Capel Minor made a terrible hash of things and belted the ball yards over the bar. As the ball disappeared into the Kop, the Chesterfield fan said, to no one in particular, 'Nepotism. Bloody nepotism.' It was greeted with silence because no one understood what he had said. It was only when I got home and looked in the dictionary that I realised what a gem it had been.

But all that changed long ago and it's no good yearning for what's disappeared. Lord Taylor wasn't required to change the game I grew up with. He had to deal with what it had become – out of date, out of touch and dangerous. The most difficult job will be to rehouse and reshape soccer while remembering to whom it really belongs. We who grew up on the terraces had it by right. The big question is – can it be given back by design?

April 1992

CEC McCORMACK –
BREAKING THE MOULD

IN THE DAYS when bungs were no bigger than the toe-cap on a player's boot and George Graham's 'gift' would have bought the entire England soccer team plus Wembley Stadium, we had a centre-forward at Barnsley, Cec McCormack, who was as good at his job as any I have seen.

He joined us from Middlesbrough in 1951 and it must be said there were a few who, when they saw him, wondered if the manager hadn't made a mistake. There wasn't much of him; he was short and frail looking with wispy blond hair.

In those days, centre-forwards were big bullocking men with foreheads like Herman Munster and legs that would comfortably support a full-sized billiard table. They were put on this earth to kick centre-halves and to fill the net with footballs and goalkeepers. Their reputations were such that when they walked down the street, people stepped aside to let them by and they never paid to get into the local dancehall.

So it was a shock when we saw Cecil McCormack. He answered our doubts by scoring 33 goals in 37 league games, setting a club record that still stands. He was skilful, graceful and two-footed. He wasn't big enough to dominate in the air but, as he said, he used his head for thinking with.

Anyone who watched Barnsley in that period will tell you about the day McCormack scored five against Luton Town. Bernard Streten, who played for England, was in goal. Syd Owen, who also won a cap or two, was centre-half. Forty years on and I can still see McCormack's third goal as he flowed past two defenders and drove the ball into the roof of the net. The net did 'bulge', the goalkeeper was a 'hapless custodian'. All the clichés of the day were confirmed and remain in my mind.

No one knew him well. I once followed him from the ground to the snooker hall and waited outside but it started to rain so I went home. It was said he liked a drink and that he would sometimes tell the dressing room that he fancied scoring a goal or two today, and was always as good as his word.

He went as soon as he came. We transferred him to Notts County where he played alongside Tommy Lawton. We sold him for £20,000 and a young lad called Tommy Taylor took his place. McCormack emigrated to Canada, where he played with Toronto All Stars. That was the last I heard of him until I was told the other day that he had died.

I always tell people he was one of the best and I mean it. I remember the line in the Barnsley programme that summed him up: 'Against West Ham McCormack scored his customary goal.'

March 1995

BATTLING BARNSLEY RISE FROM PITS TO ATTAIN THEIR PLACE IN THE SUN

I DON'T KNOW how we survived it, me and Dickie Bird. There was a point in the second half, with Bradford getting on top, when I seriously thought he might invade the pitch and bring them off for bad light. When the second goal went in and we knew we were there we didn't say much because had we done so I think we might have shed a tear. Silly, isn't it, how the love of a team makes grown men foolish. Why do we feel that way?

I was five when I was first taken to Oakwell. At first I stood in the front row, chin on the concrete wall into which my beloved Skinner delivered his bruised opponents. Later, as I grew taller, it became more of a problem to persuade people to let me through. My father devised a brilliant scheme whereby I put on a terrible limp and he would appeal to the spectators' better nature by crying, 'Make way, can't you see the poor little lad's got a bad leg.'

The day I stood alongside the men was a big moment in my life. The day I stood behind them because I had outgrown them was an important rite of passage. In those days my ambition was to buy a house opposite the players' entrance. It was my intention to live there with either Rita Hayworth or Vera Hruba Ralston to give me something to do when Barnsley were playing away. Fifty years on and I'm still thinking of making an offer on that house, although Rita and Vera are both sadly unavailable.

There is no known cure. During the six-day war in the Middle East, when I was pretending to be a war correspondent, I was also writing a weekly column about sport. At the height of the conflict, I found myself handing the Israeli censor an article about Skinner Normanton and the Barnsley team of my youth. There were a certain number of 'Ayups' and 'Tha'whats' in the article which the censor, a professor of English at Tel Aviv University, was certain were coded messages about Israeli troop movements. Moreover, he refused to accept my explanation that Skinner Normanton was a real name and made me delete all references to my hero. He was convinced I was working for British intelligence.

I told Skinner this story some time later when we were brought together in a television studio. When I had finished he thought for a moment and then said, 'There wasn't many Barnsley supporters in Israel, then?'

Because of my passion for the club and the players of my youth, Sidney Albert Normanton gained a fame beyond the parish boundaries. Making a speech in Darwin, Australia, I was introduced as 'the man who made Clogger Normanton famous'. This information made little impact on the audience, who didn't have a clue what the man was talking about. But I did and although Skinner would have objected to being called

'Clogger' – he always thought of himself as competitive rather than crude – I wondered, not for the first time, what it was about the name that captured the imagination of strangers.

I came to the conclusion it was because they thought Skinner was an adjective as well as a nickname. It summed up for them the kind of man who came up the shaft in his pit muck, pulled on a Barnsley shirt and went out to give people a taste of what it was like to play against a Yorkshire collier. After all, the teams were, and still are, called 'Battling Barnsley'.

While it is true a fair number of hard men have spilled blood at Oakwell, it must always be remembered that Normanton's midfield partner for a while was Danny Blanchflower, and that the Barnsley teams of the forties and fifties played their football on the carpet. Danny Wilson's present team play the same way. The other Danny would have approved. He was a purist and a hard man to please.

Danny Blanchflower was an important influence in my life. He was the first player who made me want to write about the game. He had a style and intelligence that isolated him from hoi polloi. Sometimes we would stand outside the ground and get the players' autographs after training and then, like lovelorn swains, follow them to the snooker hall where they spent the afternoons. I don't know why we followed them. We knew where they were going. One day Danny walked past the snooker hall and continued up the hill to the technical college. He was studying economic theory.

The Barnsley team of that time were as pleasant and skilful a combination as I have seen. Pat Kelly was an acrobat of a goalkeeper who would walk on his hands in the penalty area when he was bored. Gordon Pallister was a languid and stylish full-back who owned a temperance bar where you could buy pints of sarsaparilla. We used to go and buy a pint between three of us just to sit and gawp. Johnny Kelly was the man who changed the face of English football by giving Alf Ramsey such a towsing when Southampton played Barnsley that Alf vowed vengeance on wingers and banished them from his '66 World Cup team. They have had a hard time ever since.

Kelly's partner was a whey-faced miner from Fife called Jimmy Baxter. He played his first game for Barnsley against Manchester United. The following Monday he reported for work at Warncliffe Woodmoor Colliery. He looked like a man who lived underground on a diet of crisps and Park Drive. He was a marvellous player with more tricks than a con man and the bewitching quality of a snake charmer. He went to Preston and partnered Tom Finney. Tom said he was a footballer of the highest quality and Mr Finney (why not Sir Tom?) knew one when he saw one, being one himself.

Cec McCormack was the centre-forward who once put five past Bernard Streten of Luton Town and was reckoned by common consent to be the best goalscorer we had seen in a Barnsley shirt. Alongside him was a local youth called Tommy Taylor before he stepped across the threshold to greatness and tragedy.

Blanchflower was the creative soul of the team and for a couple of seasons turned in performances of such imagination and quality they last forever in the minds of those lucky enough to see them.

Before the game, I drove through the pit villages surrounding Barnsley. This was where I grew up so it was partly a trip down memory lane but also, and more usefully, a reminder of the community served by Barnsley Football Club. When I was a young man the link between pit and club was obvious. The only difference between player and spectator was one worked down the pit and watched Barnsley and the other worked down the pit and played for Barnsley. Nowadays the pits have gone. The slag heaps are being landscaped, the winding gear is dismantled. The generation singing Barnsley's anthem, 'It's Just Like Watching Brazil', on Saturday knows what a pit looks like but their children won't.

The ground has changed, too, with new stands, although I can't wait to hear what Manchester United fans think of our visitors accommodation, which hasn't got a roof. What is more, I would love to see Gianfranco Zola's face when he has to stand in line for a bath. We've never been big on pampering in Barnsley. I don't know what it all means because it hasn't sunk in. What I am sure of is that something special has occurred and it couldn't have happened to nicer or more deserving people.

April 1997

Danny Wilson left Barnsley in 1998 after their single season in the Premier League. He managed Sheffield Wednesday until he was sacked near the end of his second season in a forlorn attempt to stave off relegation. He resurfaced at Bristol City in 2000.

FARMER WILSON, THE
BEACON OF HOPE FOR MEN
UNDER SIEGE

I CHOSE TO WATCH Barnsley play Manchester United
at home mainly because the stand at Oakwell doesn't
have a sofa for me to hide behind. They can knock the
FA Cup all they will but I have to tell you the last time
I had comparable palpitations was the time I interviewed
Raquel Welch. The other reason I didn't make the trip
was because of what happened the last time we played
United in a Cup-tie. That was thirty-four years ago when
we lost 4–0 and I was there. The main reason was to
do with George Best. Matt had told us he was something
special and the television company I worked for asked
me to take a look with a view to a documentary. He
was seventeen at the time with short-back-and-sides and
the physique of a street urchin. I had seen more muscles
on a shoelace. It wasn't long before he demonstrated
his quality, scoring the first goal from the edge of the
box with all the insouciant certainty that became his
trademark. We made the documentary but never got
anywhere near anticipating the real impact George was
to have, not just on football but on the culture of the
sixties. George arrived, Stanley Matthews retired. It
wasn't simply a replacement, more like a revolution; but
we weren't to know it until later.

Danny Wilson, Barnsley's impressive young manager, is not much given to nostalgia but he might be interested to know I was at Oakwell that last time Barnsley beat Newcastle United in the FA Cup. It was back in the days just after the war when the competition was played in two legs. There were more than 60,000 at Newcastle for the first leg and they beat us 4–2. Jackie Milburn, of blessed memory, scored two and one of the other goalscorers was Albert Stubbins, who, as I recall, was a big red-headed lad who went on to play for Liverpool. Inside-right (they had them in those days) was Ernie Taylor, who was such a magician with a football he should have come on the field wearing a big black cloak with doves concealed about his person.

The return game at Oakwell created so much interest the local collieries voluntarily closed after acknowledging that if they didn't they would be unable to operate, because most of their workforce would be attending hastily arranged funerals on the day in question. More than 27,000 people stood in heavy rain to witness Barnsley achieve the impossible with a 3–0 victory. As I write I imagine I can smell the crowd: a mixture of Woodbines, Barnsley Bitter, Brylcreem and damp. We had a centre-half called Joe 'Farmer' Wilson who scored a goal and played the game of his life. Such was the difference between his performance against Newcastle and his usual effort there ought to have been a stewards' inquiry. He had a butterfly's glory. Next season he had gone and we bought a centre-half called Stan Charlesworth from Grimsby. He cost £6,500, which in those days was a fortune. In fact, I remember working it out that if 27,000 fans paid £3,000 at the gate for the Newcastle game, which they did (those were the days) then Charlesworth was worth 60,000 paying customers.

This was heady stuff. In his first game against Bradford Park Avenue, he scored spectacularly through his own goal. He proved such a danger in the penalty area that in subsequent matches our centre-forward, George Robledo, was given the task of marking his team-mate. Charlesworth lasted seven games and then disappeared into non-league football.

None of this will make much difference when we take on Newcastle this time round except to say we did it once and we can do it again. And if we can't, then the journey so far has lasted longer than all except the most optimistic fan could have imagined.

It may well be that Mr Wilson and his team do not survive this season in the Premier League. They have discovered, as all promoted teams do, a world of difference between promotion and staying up. Danny Wilson said he wished he could start the season about now, having deduced what it takes to survive in the Premier League. As it is he, his team and their supporters have demonstrated good nature in the face of adversity. They might have been walloped now and then on the field of play but have never sought refuge in blaming others, like some I could mention with more money and less dignity.

It says much for their demeanour that even if they do go down, their reputation will be enhanced. Two things

I remember from the euphoria when Barnsley knew they were promoted. The first was John Dennis, the club chairman, saying that whatever happened in the Premier League they must be determined to enjoy it. The second was Mr Dennis being embraced by a fan in a bear hug and saying to me over his worshipper's shoulder, 'Next season if we go down he'll be calling me a pillock.' On the evidence so far, Mr Dennis has been as good as his word in the first instance and after what happened on Wednesday night might well have got the second part wrong; or at least, delayed it for a season or two.

March 1998

SKINNER

CUP-TIES were different from other games. If Barnsley won we went to the pictures in the best seats, but if they lost there was sometimes a punch-up and the old man would come home from the boozer with a skinful saying the beer was off.

Barnsley, of course, used to be a good Cup-fighting side. They only won the Cup once and that was in 1912, but they've never forgotten it and many a team from a higher division has been slain by them on that ground with the muck stacks peeping over the paddock. The reason for Barnsley's success in the Cup was, more often than not, that their game remained unchanged throughout years of tactical innovation. The team was both blind and deaf to subtleties like the bolt defence, the wall pass, 4-2-4 and deep-lying centre-forwards. Their game was founded rock solid on two basic principles best summed up by the exhortations of their supporters to 'Get stuck in' or, alternatively, 'Get rid'.

During one spectacular Cup run after the war, when Barnsley had beaten a First Division side, the old man held forth on the team's virtues on the bus going home. What he said was, 'They'll take some stopping, yon team. They'll kick 'owt that moves.' The bus agreed.

This love of hard combative graft above all else was not in any way unique among the supporters who Saturday after Saturday had their weekend-end mood dictated by how their team fared. Their unanimous favourites were the hard men who got stuck in and got rid without thought for the game's niceties. The odd sophisticates who crept into the team were tolerated but never loved. Thus they will tell you even now that Danny Blanchflower once played for Barnsley, but that he wasn't a patch on Skinner Normanton.

Normanton, I suppose, personified Barnsley's Cup-fighting qualities. He was tough, tireless, aggressive, with a tackle as swift and spectacular as summer lightning. In the family tree of football his grandfather was Wilf Copping, his godson is Nobby Stiles. And just in case anyone is still uncertain about what kind of player he was, he could claim a distant link with Rocky Marciano. He was a miner and built like one. Billiard-table legs and a chest like the front of a coal barge. He was so fearsome that there are those who will tell you that naughty children in and around Barnsley were warned by their parents, 'If you don't be good we'll send for Skinner.'

The other legend about him, probably equally true, was that certain inside-forwards of delicate constitution were known to develop nervous rashes and mysterious stomach disorders when faced with the prospect of a Saturday afternoon's sport with Skinner in opposition.

Cup-ties were his speciality, inside-forwards with international reputations were his meat. He clinched one game for Barnsley in a manner all his very own. There was about ten minutes to go, the scores level, and Barnsley were awarded a penalty. The inside-forward placed the ball on the spot and as he turned to walk back Skinner, from the halfway line, set off running. The inside-forward, ready to turn to take the kick, saw Skinner approaching like an odds-on favourite and wisely stepped aside. From that moment the grey, dour ground was lit with the purple and gold of pure fantasy. Without slackening speed, Skinner kicked the ball with his toe-end. And, as he did, many things happened – the bar started shaking and humming, the goalkeeper fell to his face stunned and the ball appeared magically in the back of the net. What in fact had happened was that Skinner's shot had struck the underside of the crossbar, rebounded on to the back of the goalkeeper's neck, flattened him and ricocheted into the goal.

Barnsley, by virtue of Skinner's genius in scoring with the penalty and at the same time reducing the opponents to ten men, won the game.

It was soon after, though, that Skinner for the first and last time met his match. Again it was a Cup-tie and this time Barnsley were playing Arsenal at Highbury. Going down on the train with the crates of light ale under the seat, we agreed that if Skinner could frighten them Barnsley had a chance. But we didn't know that Arsenal had someone just as hard as Skinner and twice as clever. His name was Alec Forbes and Barnsley lost. Going sadly home, we agreed with the thought that if Barnsley had Forbes they'd soon get into the First Division. What we left unsaid was that they'd probably make it by default because other teams faced with the prospect of playing against a side containing both

Skinner and Forbes would probably give Barnsley two points to stop at home.

Anyway things have changed now. Skinner has retired and there's no one to take his place. The last time I saw Barnsley in a Cup-tie things were different. They played Manchester United at Barnsley and went down ever so politely 4–0. United played as if they had written the modern theory of the game and Barnsley as if they'd read it backwards. There were no fights either on or off the field, Denis Law shimmered like quicksilver and scored as he pleased, and a young lad called George Best played with the instinctive joy of a genius. There was only one flash of the old fighting spirit. As Law cheekily and magically dribbled round the wing-half, stopped, showed him the ball, then beat him again, a bloke standing near us shouted, 'Tha' wouldn't have done that to Skinner, Denis.' Those who remembered smiled. But knowingly.

Irresistible name that captured the imagination worldwide

Skinner Normanton died peacefully aged sixty-eight. Between 1947 and 1953 he played 134 times for Barnsley and ended his career with a brief spell at Halifax. He retired to his garden where he grew sunflowers and turned out occasionally for the local team when they were a man short.

Sydney Albert Normanton was a local legend when he played at Barnsley. He was the hard man of the side, the minder for ball-playing colleagues of delicate disposition. There wasn't much of him but every ounce counted. He was destructive in the tackle, as unrelenting as a heat-seeking missile in pursuit of the enemy.

If I close my eyes I see two images. The first is a still photograph with Skinner posed in the manner of the day, arms folded and one foot on the leather football. His hair was short and wavy, parted near the middle and rigid with Brylcreem, and his legs were as sturdy as pit-props with bulging shin pads and bulbous toe-caps that glowed with dubbin and menace.

My second memory is more like a black and white film of the time. Skinner took a penalty in a Cup-tie and ran from the halfway line before toe-ending the sodden football. The ball became a blur as it passed the motionless goalkeeper, crashing into the underside of the crossbar and rebounded on to the back of the goalkeeper's head and into the net. The goalkeeper was poleaxed and took several minutes to recover and it wasn't until much later that the iron crossbar stopped quivering from the impact of the shot. For a while it hummed like a male voice choir.

He was a local celebrity. Mothers would tell their children to stop mucking about or they would send for Skinner. He gained a wider audience many years after he retired when I first wrote about him. I don't know what it was about the article that captured the imagination. I think it might have been the name. If you wanted to invest a local football hero of the time, someone who worked in the pits during the week and spent Saturday afternoons kicking lumps off the opposition, you'd invent a man called something like Skinner Normanton.

Whatever the reason may have been, his fame extended far beyond his beloved Oakwell. There used to be a Skinner Normanton Appreciation Society in Kuala Lumpur, and I have been asked about him during all my travels throughout the world. There was something in the name that was irresistible to Brits living abroad,

particularly when they were feeling homesick for Saturday afternoons and kick-off time.

Many people believed him to be a mythical character like The Great Wilson of the *Wizard*. I remember Yorkshire Television producing him as a surprise guest on a programme I was doing in Leeds. They brought him into the studio and announced him in a triumphant fashion as if they had found Lord Lucan or were about to produce the Loch Ness monster on the end of a lead.

He was smaller than I remembered and was wearing a blue suit with a nipped-in waist. The hair was as immaculate as ever and he looked like he was going to church. I had never seen him in his Sunday best. When he spoke his voice was soft, the manner modest, even shy. It was difficult to convince people that this gentle and diffident man had at one time put the fear of God up any member of the human race who didn't wear a Barnsley shirt. Well, that's not strictly true. Sometimes even his own team-mates were victims of Skinner's fierce competitive spirit – he was once sent off by the manager in a practice game. Danny Blanchflower played a season or two with Skinner, but there wasn't room for both of them at Oakwell. For a while Skinner fretted in the reserves while Blanchflower began a journey that ended in the pantheon. Skinner settled for something less but there will be many who didn't know him, nor ever saw him play, who will mourn him.

He played at a time when the game drank deep from its tap roots and although there were many more skilled and talented than he, there was no one who better represented what you were up against if you took on a collier from Barnsley.

I was thinking that they ought to name the new stand at Barnsley after him. The Skinner Normanton stand would be a constant reminder that no matter how much we merchandise the modern game we must always remember what it is we are really selling. Nowadays they talk of image. There was a time, when Skinner was a lad, when it had a soul.

May 1995

FIFTIES
NOSTALGIA

Nostalgia is not what it was before video

I AM AS NOSTALGIC as the next man but I doubt that I will sacrifice six hours of my life tonight to watch BBC2's so-called celebration of soccer. The trouble with nostalgia is it starts with the invention of the video tape. Everything that went before is left to old men on park benches and grandads telling stories.

The major misconception of the television generation is that if it isn't on video it didn't happen. 'The 100 Best Goals Ever Scored' is a misnomer. It is, in fact, 'The 100 Best Goals Ever Seen On Television', a different proposition altogether.

It does not, for instance, include the goal scored by Jimmy Baxter in the third round of the FA Cup at Leeds Road, Huddersfield, in January 1947. Baxter was what journalists used to delight in describing as 'a ball-playing inside-forward'. He was so frail that he looked like he ought to be in the care of the local authority. His physical condition was attributed to stunted growth brought about by an addiction to Woodbines. Such was his habit, he would light up at half-time in the dressing room. When he left Barnsley and joined Preston North End, the cameras visited Deepdale to capture Tom Finney for 'This Is Your

Life'. Baxter was discovered lying in the team bath having a smoke.

In those days, Huddersfield Town played in the First Division. They had a team built round the incomparable talents of Peter Doherty. He was as good a player as I ever saw – inventive, combative, tireless. When he joined Raich Carter at Derby, the two of them, all too briefly, formed one of the great inside-forward combinations.

At Huddersfield, Doherty played alongside Vic Metcalfe, a stylish left-winger of great skill, with a left foot so accurate and reliable that it should have been used to deliver registered post. Jimmy Glazzard was the centre-forward. There wasn't much of him but what there was consisted mainly of forehead flattened through years of contact with sodden leather footballs aimed by Metcalfe's left boot.

The score was 3–3 with ten minutes to go when Baxter scored a goal of such wit and imagination it has remained in my mind ever since. He was about thirty yards out and dawdling on the ball, as players were allowed to do in those days, when he looked up and saw that the Huddersfield goalkeeper, Bob Hesford, had strayed off his line. Baxter flicked the ball up and lobbed it goalwards. It had the height and trajectory of a sand wedge hit high and soft to the pin.

As soon as the ball left Baxter's boot, Hesford knew that he was in trouble. He started back-pedalling with his eye on the ball until he reached the point where the angle of his head went beyond the point of balance. Then he toppled backwards into his own net, arms flailing, like a man falling back over a steep cliff. He arrived at the goalline at about the same time as Baxter's lob.

I couldn't begin to count the number of goals I have seen scored since that January day all those many years ago, but none remains in my mind. I think it had something to do with the tempo of the moment, the fact it seemed to happen in slow motion. It was artful and clever. It was also witnessed by a child madly in love with soccer, many years before the taste of the game became sour on his palate.

What I also remember about that day is that, as Barnsley battled to hang on and win the match, a fan presented the Barnsley goalkeeper with an alarm clock so that he might put it in the back of the net along with his cap and gloves and know how long there was to go. It was a charming and humorous gesture and typical of an age before soccer lost its innocence.

Not that Jimmy Baxter was a babe in arms. He was no oil painting. Indeed, he played the aforesaid game at Huddersfield with a broken jaw, unknown to his team-mates. They couldn't tell there was anything wrong by looking at him. As he weighed just over nine stone, any lump appearing on his person was taken as a welcome sign that he was putting on weight.

He was physically so unlike an athlete that if he played today he would be in regular demand by shrewd television casting directors. Imagine him in those television commercials where the Gary Linekers of the game are seen eating cereal and looking brimmingly healthy.

Consider the fun to be had if the Lineker figure said to the camera, 'If you don't eat your cereal then this is what can happen,' and we see Jimmy Baxter, looking as if he was on his last legs, wolfing down bacon, eggs and fried bread with a full ashtray on the table next to the bottle of brown sauce.

There's little doubt that if Jimmy Baxter turned up at a club nowadays and asked for a trial he would be shown the door. If they let him inside, he would fail the medical. It would be a grievous mistake because he was a tough little so-and-so who could mix it with the biggest and the roughest. I once saw him topple Derek Dooley in spectacular fashion at Barnsley. A couple of weeks before, I had seen Dooley at Hillsborough terrify the Middlesbrough defenders into giving him the freedom of the park.

For those who never saw him play, Dooley was a tall and strong centre-forward who feared no man and had the single-minded thrust of a rat up a pump. He scored 62 goals in 61 appearances for Wednesday before he was tragically injured and forced to leave the game. He was greatly assisted in his goal-scoring feats by a considerable footballer called Redfern Froggatt who would send Dooley careering towards goal with meticulous and inviting long passes. There was nothing Dooley liked more than a straight gallop on goal and there were few keepers around who relished the prospect of coming face to face with 13 stone of highly motivated bone and muscle.

When Sheffield Wednesday came to Barnsley, our

keeper, Harry Hough, threw himself at Dooley's feet and suffered a broken arm. Shortly after, our centre-half confronted Mr Dooley and thereafter spent the rest of the game doing a passable imitation of Long John Silver. It was with his team reduced to nine men that Baxter, having already scored two goals, decided to come to the rescue.

Now I am not going to swear to what happened but let me tell you what I think I saw. Baxter, who had dropped deep to look after Dooley, gained the ball near the corner flag in his own half of the field and invited the centre-forward to advance. As Dooley approached, arms outstretched, hemming Baxter in, the little man stepped over the ball and headed Dooley in the goolies. There were some who later claimed that Baxter was so small he had to jump to make contact, but that is clearly fanciful.

Over the years I have replayed the incident over and over in my mind and the only conclusion I can be sure of is that whatever happened caused Dooley to lose interest in proceedings for quite a time. Then, as now, the referee didn't see anything and even had he done so I doubt if he would have believed it.

Had Baxter played in the video era, I have no doubt that he would have featured in a large chunk of tonight's programme. Similarly, as part of tonight is also devoted to goalkeepers and their foibles, I have little doubt that several custodians of my youth would have featured strongly, particularly a Barnsley keeper called Pat Kelly who regularly patrolled his goalmouth while walking on his hands. One day an enterprising opponent tried a shot from his own half having seen that Kelly was upside down on the penalty spot. Kelly saw the ball coming and caught it between his knees.

Now you can believe that or not. The point is I was there and you weren't and neither was a television camera. The trouble with video evidence is that it stops people elaborating on past events. It means that my children won't be able to wax nostalgic to their children like I did to them. You might regard this as a more honest approach and therefore a healthier state of affairs. I don't. The trouble with a newsreel approach to life is that it denies romance. It is also death to the imagination.

May 1994

Treasured memories
are making way for
cold cash

I T WAS a week when Arthur Rowley put his medals
up for sale and Manchester United announced profits
of £11 million; a time to consider where football has
come from and where it is going. Rowley played for
Fulham, West Brom, Leicester and Shrewsbury. He
scored 434 goals in 619 games, breaking Dixie Dean's
Football League record of 379 goals and Jimmy
McGrory's British record of 410. The footballs with
which he achieved both records will be part of the sale,
as will two Second Davison championship medals he
won with Leicester in the Fifties.

Arthur Rowley is sixty-eight. He said he was selling
his mementos 'because they are just lying about, so I
might as well enjoy what they are worth.' It is sad, is it
not, that a player whose record will never be beaten,
who occupies his own special place in the Hall of Fame,
finds it necessary to part with the rewards of his talent.
There should be a law proclaiming that sporting heroes
never feel the need to sell their trophies. They should
be allowed to dwell in that part of our memory where
they are forever young and strong and always – as the
reporters of the time described it – 'bulging the net'.

Arthur Rowley was particularly good at scoring goals

– none better – and he has the record to prove it. He was a burly man with a straight parting in wavy hair. No matter how wet the day nor how many times his forehead came into contact with the heavy leather ball, he was never seen with a hair out of place.

We had a centre-forward at Barnsley called Cec McCormack who could play in a mud heap during a thunderstorm and leave the field without a mark on his person, his shorts still dry. My theory was that he played three feet above the park. He was my hero, so anything was possible.

For all his ability at scoring goals, Rowley never gained a full England cap. The fact is he operated in the forties and fifties at a time when there were one or two good centre-forwards about. The goalscorer's job in those days was much less complicated than it is today. Modern strikers are expected to defend, work in midfield and run up and down either flank as well as score goals. In the days of Rowley, Lawton, Lofthouse and Ardron, leading the line was the equivalent of being front horse in a cavalry charge. Goalkeepers had not yet become a protected species. Nowadays, if a keeper holds the ball he is safe. When Arthur Rowley and his like prowled the penalty area and centre-forwards were allowed to charge the keeper and bundle him over the line when he had the ball, catching the ball meant his problems had only just begun. I once saw Wally Ardron force Cliff Binns, our goalkeeper, plus two covering defenders, into the net at Barnsley. Wally wasn't born, he was forged in a Rotherham steelworks.

Derek Dooley who played for Sheffield Wednesday before an accident caused his retirement, was another who created fear and panic. I once saw him fasten on to a through ball and charge towards the Middlesbrough goal, which was manned by a flamboyant character called Rolando Ugolini. It was, I suppose, a fifty-fifty ball. The odds changed dramatically in Dooley's favour when Rolando stepped aside and waved him on, rather like a stationmaster standing on the platform watching the Master Cutler hurtle through.

Some keepers chose more drastic methods. Chesterfield had a keeper called Ray Middleton who specialised in punching away crosses. He had one fist for the ball and the other in reserve for any centre-forward brave enough to meet the challenge. Nowadays the modern keeper is a popinjay in a multicoloured jersey, the striker a nimble crafty predator.

The changes that have occurred between the careers of Arthur Rowley and Alan Shearer provide a rich area for anthropologists and historians alike and can be seen as natural developments in working-class culture. What happens to the game in the next ten years will, I suspect, be a lot more difficult and complicated to explain in terms of a people's pastime with working-class heroes.

Football is setting off on an adventure with limitless horizons in terms of global development and riches. The few will know wealth beyond their wildest imaginings; the rest will come to terms with eating crumbs from the rich man's table or perish. The fact is the gap between Arthur Rowley and the future of football is that between a bus and a limousine, a pittance and a fortune, a sport and an industry. In the final analysis, it is the difference between keeping your medals and selling them.

October 1994

Nostalgia: the disease with no known cure

BACK to Oakwell, the cradle of my nostalgia. The home of Barnsley Football Club has changed, and for the better. The last time I visited, it was still possible to stand in the spot where I had always stood. Now it is occupied by a seat. Opposite my vantage point was a low shed and beyond that a view of pithead gear and distant hills. In its place is a handsome new stand which cost less than Stan Collymore but more than Tommy Taylor whom we sold to Manchester United for £29,999; he made Collymore look like a selling plater.

There I go again. Nostalgia is football's version of mad cow disease. It is brought about by close contact with the product and there is no known cure; or is it genetic, like madness and going bald? My father was a lifelong nostalgic. He settled any argument about football by saying, 'He wasn't as good as Pongo.' Pongo Waring was a centre-forward of eccentric nature and brilliant gifts who played for Aston Villa before joining Barnsley the year I was born.

There was a time when nostalgia became a dirty word. The fanzine generation with its Year Zero approach to football would have none of it. I am delighted to see it making a comeback. Television is awash with football nostalgia although much of it, I fear, is based on a fascination for fashion rather than any deep desire to learn from the history of the game.

It is a good time for football to remember where it came from. The game has changed more dramatically over the past decade than at any time in its history and with the change has come uncertainty and confusion. It was once possible to plot the development of football for ten years ahead and not be made to look foolish. Only a madman would endeavour to draw up a blueprint for the next decade except to say (hopefully) that I will still be stopping conversations with, 'If you think he could play football you never saw Tom Finney.' Or, 'Don't talk to me about hard men. What about Skinner Normanton?'

Football grounds are the vaults of our memories. As I stood in the back of the new stand looking down on the pitch, the images of the past came together, faded and reassembled like the patterns in a kaleidoscope. I could see Danny Blanchflower floating the ball into the path of Gavin Smith who, in full stride, was more or less unstoppable. When they opened the gate by the corner flag for him to run through, there was nothing to stop him until he reached the main road. Nowadays

he would end up in the souvenir shop after demolishing sixty rows of seats.

Smith went and Arthur Kaye took over. There were few better wingers in British football. He was a tough, aggressive, fighting-cock of a man. We sold him to Blackpool for £13,500 which these days would probably be his weekly wage. There was a time in the early fifties when he would cross the ball into the goalmouth for Taylor to cause havoc.

Taylor was as good a centre-forward as I have seen. He was tall, two-footed and a memorably graceful athlete. There have been few better headers of a football. He had Tommy Lawton's trick of seeming to float in the air while waiting to head the ball. After he joined Manchester United he played for England before perishing at Munich.

Taylor was at the cinema when a message appeared on screen: 'Tommy Taylor, please report to Oakwell.' When he arrived at the ground, Matt Busby was waiting to sign him. Matt knocked a pound off the agreed fee because he didn't want Taylor lumbered with the tag of being a £30,000 footballer. It was generally assumed that he signed for Manchester United because Busby offered the better inducement. Matt later told me that all Tommy Taylor asked for in his negotiations were tickets for his family to home matches. He was paid £15 a week.

But then that was big money for someone who had worked at the pit before becoming a professional footballer. He came from a poor mining family. He went to school with Dickie Bird, and Dickie remembers the day when Tommy was sent home because he didn't have any boots and turned up to play for the school wearing plimsolls.

Dickie said he spent hours with his mate crossing the ball so he could practise his heading. 'He used to hang there in mid-air like he was treading water,' he said. 'I've never seen anyone who could jump like he could.'

Nostalgia might dwell on things past but it makes them seem like next-door neighbours rather than visitors from a distant land. There's much to be said for it. And the wondrous quality of nostalgia is that it is unchallengeable. Like beauty, it rests in the eye of the beholder.

October 1995

HALL OF FAME REQUIRED
TO HONOUR FORGOTTEN
HEROES OF YESTERYEAR

R ETURNING to my well-worn theme of they don't
know they're born, let us consider the type of footballs they play with nowadays. We used to call them
'caseys'. Don't ask me why. The best guess is because
they were made of a bladder encased in a stout leather
outer case. They were much prized in my youth because
they were expensive. One ball would have to last a
season played, in the main, on a surface that had only
a nodding acquaintance with grass.

In those days, the same thrift was apparent at Barnsley
FC. One ball kicked out of the ground was a problem,
two a disaster. Play was held up until the ball was
retrieved by a lad on a bike; nor do I exaggerate when
I declare that the modern player in his soft leather boots
would suffer a broken foot if he kicked one of our balls.

Don't get me on the subject of boots. We couldn't
afford a pair a year so we had to buy them two sizes
too big and stuff the toes with paper until we grew into
them. Missionaries from the south were bemused at the
sight of ten years olds wearing size nine boots. They
thought they had come upon some strange tribe of
mutants with oversized feet.

We couldn't afford to be concerned with fashion. One

season when we didn't have any shirts we persuaded our mothers to knit the team kit. They were given a free hand with left-over bits of wool and when we took to the field, there wasn't one of us wearing a shirt of the same colour. We were nicknamed 'Bassetts' because we looked like Liquorice Allsorts.

Our precious ball was cared for by our team captain, whose mother loved him so much that she used to wash it and peg it on the line to dry. Halfway through the season a panel would split and the bladder would bulge through in a bleb. Fortunately, one of our team's father was a cobbler, and he used to stitch the seam. When the split became a tear he would cover it with a leather patch. Inevitably, as the ball became increasingly damaged and repaired, it lost its shape. For some reason it always came to resemble a large egg. When this happened, you just prayed to God that when you went to head the ball, it wasn't the sharp end coming towards you. It took a brave man equipped with a tungsten skull to head those balls without suffering serious injury.

When we talk of great headers of the ball from those days, we are talking of heroes, tough guys who could batter down oak doors with their foreheads. My old man said the two best headers of a ball he ever saw were Dixie Dean and Pongo Waring. He told me he saw Pongo run the length of the pitch bouncing the ball on his head before deliberately heading over an open goal because he was in dispute with the manager. Mind you, my old man was a bigger liar than Tom Pepper, unlike his son.

The best headers I ever saw were John Charles (who was also one of the best players), Tommy Lawton, Beaumont Asquith and Tony Hateley, father of Mark. Hateley senior was so proficient in the air and so useless on the ground I once suggested that at dead-ball situations his team-mates grab him by the ankles and swing him round like a seven iron so that his brow could be used to chip balls into the area. This idea is not as far-fetched as it seems, because in the days of consistent contact with heavy balls, all the great centre-forwards had foreheads with a few degrees of loft.

Beaumont Asquith, for instance, who played for Barnsley in the forties, had a brow of such noble proportions that he was nicknamed 'Beethoven' by the fans; at least by those of us who knew Beethoven wasn't one of Mr Asquith's whippets, which he bred when he wasn't heading footballs. He once scored a hat-trick of headers and had that gift of perfect timing which enabled him to outjump much taller defenders. When he was asked the secret of his heading ability, he put it down to the fact that he had a very big head. It was so large that for a bet he went to the headquarters of the country's leading hat-makers and they didn't have anything on the premises to fit him.

For a time he had a milk round in Barnsley. Those were the days when you could buy a dozen eggs or a pint of milk from your heroes and there was always the possibility of sitting next to them on the bus going to the match.

Beau Asquith was a quality footballer as felicitous on

the ground as he was powerful in the air. He could also kick with both feet, a skill seemingly beyond most of today's players who are paid more in a week than Asquith earned in a lifetime. On the other hand, not many of today's stars know how to breed greyhounds or drive a milk float. Just what they do with their spare time baffles me.

Tommy Lawton was said to hang in the air after he had jumped. It is not possible, yet the great Nijinsky, when asked the secret of his 'grand leap', said, 'Well, you jump and at the top of your jump . . . you wait a little.' That is exactly what Lawton appeared to do, except that after 'waiting a little' he would head the ball towards goal with greater power and accuracy than many others could manage with their feet. Shearer is the nearest to Lawton in the modern game; smaller and not as dominant in the air, but blessed with the same athleticism, speed and willingness to operate in the painful area of this craft.

Malcolm Allison says that when he played against Lawton the centre-forward was nearing the end of his career and yet when he jumped for a header his boots were level with Allison's chest. Allison says he could leap above the crossbar and was the best header of the ball he had ever seen.

Allison tells a poignant story of Lawton standing at a bus stop in Nottingham in the pouring rain when Mark Hateley drove past in an expensive car. It wasn't Hateley's fault he earned enough to own a posh car, but Lawton and his generation were robbed blind by

a pernicious conspiracy between clubs and football's executive.

Like many, Lawton sold off his memorabilia to subsidise his old age. When he died his son broadcast an appeal for one of his father's twenty-three caps to be returned to the family so that it might be placed on his coffin.

We are negligent with our sporting heroes. Soccer, awash with money, ought to consider spending something on remembering the past. A Hall of Fame would do. Not some tired waxworks in Lytham St Anne's or the like, but a proper celebration of the game's history and its heroes. The logical question after Tommy Lawton's family had to borrow one of his caps from a private collector is why the Football Association didn't have one. Do the FA own one of Tom Finney's caps, or Stanley Matthews' right boot? What about the shirt Bobby Moore won the World Cup in? Do the FA have that in safekeeping for the nation?

Anyone with a working knowledge of Lancaster Gate will know the answer. But if the FA have a role to play in the modern game that isn't as footling as it sometimes appears, it must surely be as the guardians of the game's heritage. Football has a fascinating history extending beyond the story of a mere game. It is time we celebrated that fact along with the people who helped shape it. Instead of Wilf Mannion feeling rejected and forgotten in Middlesbrough, he should know there is one place he has left an indelible footprint in the sand.

In many ways the FA's indifference to the game's past

is even more significant than their incoherence about its future. At least the Professional Footballers Association purchased Billy Wright's 100th cap at a recent auction and chief executive Gordon Taylor has been persuaded for some time about the need for a Hall of Fame.

Between them, these two powerful organisations ought to be able to create something football can be proud of. It would be useful, too, if it was achieved without the commercial taint which traduces so much of the game's product. For example, there is a suggestion that FIFA might create its own Hall of Fame in EuroDisney. Gordon Taylor is horrified. 'Tom Finney and Stanley Matthews standing next to Goofy and Mickey Mouse? Don't think so,' he said. Quite right. Having Paul Gascoigne under the same roof will be bad enough. There has to be a better venue – Wembley, for instance.

I would be more supportive of Wembley continuing as our national stadium if it housed a fitting celebration of our national game. By that I mean the best museum of football anywhere in the world. Then there would be no need to beg from private collectors to commemorate a giant like Tommy Lawton. Visitors would be able to inspect the kind of ball he used to play with, as well as the kit he played in, and wonder at his skill and courage, not to mention his strength in jumping so high in what today's players would regard as a pair of diver's boots.

There should also be a reconstruction of backstreets with outside closets and goals chalked on walls where artists like Carter, Mannion, Finney, Matthews, Lawton *et al* learned their skills. Today's players should be made

to pay a visit in order to learn the meaning of dedication. What is more, there ought to be a special display of a 'casey' with a bleb in it, just so you will know I wasn't making it up.

December 1996

FLAT CAPS CAN HELP
FROZEN PLAYERS ACHIEVE
THE HEIGHTS OF FASHION

A M I alone in thinking it strange that footballers with shaven heads try to keep warm by wearing gloves? Have they not been told about heat escaping upwards. If they can wear gloves, tights, cycle shorts and (for all we know) fur-lined jockstraps, what is it stop them keeping their heads warm? A flat cap would be one possibility.

I played for several years in the Barnsley and District Backyard League with several sportsmen who favoured flat hats on the field of play, most particularly 'Nebber' Nuttall. He was a centre-forward of legendary heading ability who, while in mid-air, was able to turn his cap back to front so his forehead and not his cap neb came in contact with the ball. He was called 'Nebber' not for this particular party piece but because when provoked he would remove his cap and use the neb to inflict grievous hurt on his opponent.

The possibility of transforming the flat cap into an offensive weapon would make it unsatisfactory for the Premier League. On the other hand, the Balaclava, apart from giving the wearer the appearance of being a member of an SAS hit squad, is an altogether more harmonious creation. It was also used in the Barnsley and District Backyard League, where it was discovered the only problems arose at dead-ball situations when unscrupulous players would twist their opponents' Balaclavas back to front as the ball was being played, thereby making them temporarily blind. This is nothing a new offence called 'Balaclava interference' and a few red cards cannot sort out.

It is an indication of the way football spills over into more and more areas of our everyday life that we are discussing a new line of winter football fashion accessories. It surely cannot be long before Nike come up with fur-lined boots. How long before a referee makes an appearance wearing a full-length astrakhan coat and a Cossack hat? And can the day be far away when the line is run by assistants dressed in matching oilskins with a flag in one hand and an umbrella in the other?

It is my considered view that the main change in the way our footballers dress for winter has been brought about by foreign players. Although it might be true that John Barnes wore gloves long before a Dutchman played for Barnsley or a Spaniard for Wigan, there is little doubt that what was once regarded as mild eccentricity of dress is nowadays accepted as part of a player's essential kit.

I knew things were changing when I heard the admirable Mr Gullit say that Signor Di Matteo was feeling the cold. This was in early August. At about the same time Juninho started wearing gloves, and not long after Señor Emerson discovered that while Whitley Bay might have its charms they were not to be compared with Copacabana beach, particularly on a wet Wednesday when it was difficult keeping the damp off your fish and chips.

Judging by his recent discomfort it would not surprise me if Emerson didn't become the first player to wear a Balaclava in the Premier League; nor would I be flabbergasted if he made his next appearance wearing a duffel coat and carrying a paraffin heater.

And if you are wondering what a Yorkshireman knows of South American footballers, let me tell you I am something of an expert. One of the first footballers I ever idolised was George Robledo, who played for Barnsley for a few seasons in the forties and was born in Chile. George was a centre-forward who, had he been born in England, would almost certainly have won many international honours. We transferred him to Newcastle for a few bob more than £26,000 and he became a star of the great team that won the FA Cup in '51 and '52.

These days we take South American players for granted. Forty-odd years ago, watching Robledo was a bit like having E.T. in your team. He played with men called Jack Harston, Harry Hough, Arnold Bonnell, Beaumont Asquith, Gordon Pallister and the saintly and immortal Sydney Albert Normanton. They took over from Harper, Henderson and Holley, or "'arper, 'enderson and 'olley, the 'omicidal 'orrors' as they were known, who were succeeded by Swift, Short and Sharp … the very names told visiting forwards what they might expect. Now there's a De Zeeuw in a Barnsley shirt, a Ten Heuvel and a West Indian with the glorious name of Clint Marcelle. I'm not grumbling – nor will the fans if Danny Wilson gets them into the Premier League – simply musing on how the game has changed.

There was a time when football teams found inspiration and character in the communities they represented. Now they drink from a different well. It is not so much the game itself that has changed, more that the communities have disappeared. The Barnsley team of my youth comprised men who worked down the pit and played like miners. Today the pits have closed and a way of life has passed on. What has replaced it both on and off the football field is neither better nor worse, simply different. How? Well, can you imagine Sydney Albert Normanton wearing lycra shorts and gloves? And if he did, would they ever have called him Skinner?

January 1997

Reunited with the spirit of '58 as Old Trafford performs passion play

ONE WEEK I was madly in love with Barnsley, the next I had fallen for Manchester United. How's that for an example of the glorious uncertainty of sport? You might argue that such an easy seduction simply demonstrates my fickle nature. In fact, the circumstances were so designed that I had no choice.

I reported the first game Manchester United played after the Munich air disaster. It was against Sheffield Wednesday at Old Trafford. On the park, the Sheffield Wednesday players might as well have played in ballet shoes so careful were they not to bruise their opponents or in any way offend the anguish of the multitude. It wasn't a football match. It was a demonstration of grief so profound and resonant it echoes still today. Outside Old Trafford, thousands massed in silence, muffled against the bitter cold, as if awaiting an announcement that there had been a terrible mistake and the disaster had not happened.

We didn't realise we were witnessing a resurrection of such consequence that it recruited devotees far afield from the city limits of Manchester and created one of the world's great sporting institutions.

Watching the game against Juventus last Wednesday,

absorbing the passion of the crowd, observing the magnificent stadium, I found myself remembering February 1958 and how it all started. What Sheffield Wednesday learned on that occasion, and other teams were quick to understand, was that the odds and sods managed by Jimmy Murphy neither expected nor wanted to be handled like porcelain. More often than not, this message was conveyed by Stan Crowther, a hard man signed from Aston Villa for the purpose of dissuading opponents from any outward display of sympathy.

Murphy's most significant contribution to the rebuilding of the team – apart from his own tireless energy and fierce will – was to sign Ernie Taylor from Blackpool. There wasn't much of Ernie Taylor. Nowadays he'd probably fail his medical. But what he possessed was the combative spirit of fighting bull, the cunning of a cat burglar and the kind of skills with a football that made you gibber with delight. He was what was called 'a ball-juggling inside-forward'. Once upon a time every club had one. Now they are as rare as wingers who can dribble.

His greatest ability was to unlock a defence with one pass. The distance didn't matter. Like Johnny Haynes, he had a range finder in his toe-caps. He was at the end of his career when he came from Blackpool but he had enough left in him to orchestrate a glorious finale.

Some indication of the task facing Murphy and Taylor was that when the programme was printed for the first game after the crash, the Manchester United team consisted of eleven blank spaces. Remarkably, the names Murphy fitted in around four of the players who survived – Harry Gregg, Bill Foulkes, Dennis Viollet and Bobby Charlton – took the team to Wembley. In all the history of English football, there is no story more inspiring than Murphy's achievement in getting United to the final of the FA Cup. Jimmy Murphy has never been given the accolade he deserved for enabling Manchester United's revival. He was destined to live in Busby's shadow but there is no denying the debt Sir Matt and the club owed him, even though today he is sometimes forgotten by revisionist historians.

His mouthpiece on the pitch was Taylor. In his swan song, the player cajoled, bollocked and inspired the team to Wembley. Such was his skill and self-belief that while the club were battling for survival he would conduct a tutorial, standing with his foot on the ball, sending the front-runners on their way by pointing in the direction he wanted them to go. He told Bobby Charlton, who even then liked to drop deep to collect the ball, 'When I look up, all I want to see is your arse disappearing up the field. Give me something to aim at.'

Manchester United lost at Wembley. Bolton beat them 2–0, Nat Lofthouse scoring both goals, one in controversial fashion when he bundled Harry Gregg and the ball into the back of the net. Next season – with Sir Matt back in charge – Albert Quixall arrived from Sheffield Wednesday and Ernie Taylor was on his way to Sunderland. He retired from the game in 1960 and died in 1985 aged sixty. He was some player.

It was some team he took to Wembley. It is in the

nature of things that we only remember the best of times. So whenever football fans discuss the great United teams, they generally agree there are four – three of Busby's, one created by Ferguson. There was the 1948 team who won the FA Cup and included Johnny Carey, Henry Cockburn, Jimmy Delaney, Arthur Rowley, Johnny Morris and Charlie Mitten; then the Busby Babes of Roger Byrne, Tommy Taylor, Eddie Coleman, and the incomparable Duncan Edwards. Next came the United team who won the European Cup in '68 and in Best, Law and Charlton possessed three of the greatest talents produced by Britain. Busby thought the Babes the best. He had no doubt that the pre-Munich team were about to become the best side ever. It is a tribute to Alex Ferguson that he has continued the tradition and produced a team who, on their day, can play football the equal of anything yet witnessed at Old Trafford.

It is time that Jimmy Murphy's team were included in the roll of honour. They might have lacked the glitter of the others but it would be difficult to name another who so courageously battled against overwhelming odds. More than that, they were responsible for the special link which exists to this day between Manchester United and a tribal following encircling the world. I was once in the Arctic Circle making a documentary when a peasant guarding a herd of reindeer approached. 'Manchester United,' he said, nodding in my direction. I indicated that was my name. Satisfied I knew what he was talking about, he said, 'Bobby Charlton. Number one.' So when we talk about the future of Manchester

United, let us remember the team who gave them a future to look forward to: Gregg, Foulkes, Greaves, Goodwin, Cope, Crowther, Dawson, Taylor, Charlton, Viollet, Webster.

In his autobiography *In My Way*, Sir Matt said that after Munich he vowed to keep the name of Manchester United on people's lips. He said, 'Our supporters who roared us on to Wembley immediately after the crash deserve nothing less.' Even though the club now play in more elegant and perhaps inhibiting surroundings, the crowd have not stopped roaring. Cynics argue their passion is merely a manifestation of wishful thinking, but since when has being a football fan been based on anything other than hope?

That bring us back to the glorious uncertainty of sport and how I came to support both Manchester United and Barnsley. It is axiomatic that a man cannot love two football teams in equal measure. But he can love them differently. It is the difference between obsession and admiration. For instance, as I sit in front of my radio every Saturday at 5 p.m., pen poised for the football results, I know that if Manchester United lose, I will be disappointed, but if Barnsley go down, I am distraught.

Together over the years they have given me a fairly comprehensive experience of what it is like to be a football fan. I have travelled from Old Trafford and a city in mourning to an unforgettable night at Wembley and Bobby Charlton holding the European Cup on high. At Oakwell where I could see the slag heaps in the distance when I was a kid, I saw a stripling youth called Tommy

Taylor score a hat-trick and knew he was a good 'un before Sir Matt did. Standing on the same spot, I saw one of our players, who had come straight from a shift at the pit, take a throw-in and then turn round and pinch a chip from a man in the crowd. He was hungry so he had several. It was a kind of communion.

There is no cure to being a fan. Angry and disenchanted as I am at some aspects of the game, I am unable to give it up. Whether umbilical or adoptive, the link between fan and club is a special one, far too deep to be severed even by yobs who abuse the relationship or spivs who put a price on it.

November 1996

WHEN PLAYERS FEARED TO HEAD

CURRENT RESEARCH into the effect heading a football has on the human brain is a bit late. Modern footballs are so light it must be like heading a soapsud. In any case, investigations into what goes on inside the present-day footballer's skull would be better directed towards discovering why so many appear not to have a brain at all, never mind one damaged by a football. John Hartson is but the latest in a long line. Research was needed when we played with a ball made of clog leather strong enough to withstand a season of street football. When it split and blebbed we repaired it with patches. The local cobbler was an expert. He could patch it on the inside so it didn't change shape. The do-it-yourself method was to sew a patch on to the outside of the ball so that by season's end it looked like a barnacled cannon ball.

A tactic of those days was to soak the ball in water overnight and at kick-off pass the ball back to our keeper who would belt an up and under for their centre-half to deal with. If he was brave enough to head the ball, it meant we were playing against ten men until they brought him round; and ten and a half after that because generally it took two or three hours before the head and neck emerged from between the shoulder blades which is where they disappeared after contact with the ball.

In those days you could identify the centre-halves by the shape of their foreheads. They were hammered flat by a thousand muddy balls. We had one at Barnsley called Archie Whyte who was nicknamed 'Ludwig' because he had a forehead like Beethoven. He had sleepy eyes too which we put down to watching too many Robert Mitchum movies. Now I realise he was permanently concussed.

There were several centre-halves around in those days who appeared to live on another planet. We had another who specialised in heading through his own goal and had to be marked by our centre-forward in his own penalty area. Mind you, the centre-forwards of those days were a rough lot. Not only did they spend a lifetime heading the equivalent of a medicine ball but they were expected to do so while putting ball, goalkeeper and as many opponents as possible into the net at the same time.

Two of the best I ever saw were Nat Lofthouse and Wally Ardron. Both had the single-minded aggression of fighting bulls. My father reckoned the best of all was Dixie Dean. I never saw Dean play, but my father would always say, 'Best header and he did it all with a plate in his head.'

The business about footballers having a plate upstairs was not new to me. We had a player at Barnsley, a winger of great eccentricity, who would sometimes talk to corner flags. This was explained by the generally accepted statement that the poor fellow had a plate in his head. How it got there was never discussed. In Dean's case, I later learned, he had a road accident requiring surgery involving a metal plate. It didn't slow him down. In 1927–28 he scored 60 goals in 39 league games. His prowess as a header of the ball was such that when he nodded to Elisha Scott, the Liverpool goalkeeper, in the street, Scott dived through a plate-glass window.

People say this is apocryphal although you never know with goalkeepers. They are a weird lot and Scott had some curious habits. He always wore three sweaters, even in a heatwave, and was the first footballer to wear tights; in his case, they were long johns dyed black with stitched on knee pads. In the 1920s they thought Scott was a weirdo. Nowadays he would be advertising pantyhose.

The nearest anyone has ever come to Dean's record was Derek Dooley who scored 46 goals in 39 league games for Sheffield Wednesday in 1951–52. Wednesday were in the Second Division at the time. So were Barnsley and I saw a lot of Dooley. The accident which ended in his leg being amputated was one of the tragedies of the game.

He was a large, gangling man with size 12 boots and a forehead as wide as a grand piano. Such was his power and single-minded determination it took a brave man to stand in his path. Dooley at full steam with elbows flying, knees pumping and eyes bulging could only be stopped by a defence skilled in the use of anti-tank weapons. Redfern Froggatt, an adroit distributor of the ball, would lurk until Derek started his run and then he'd direct the ball into his stride, daring the opposition to confront Dooley's momentum. When Derek scored twice against Middlesbrough, on each occasion the opposition parted like the Red Sea. But there was more to Derek Dooley than strength. He would have played for England many times had it not been for the awful accident that finished his career. He was some player.

He must wonder about a game where modern centre-forwards, who only score every Pancake Tuesday, earn more in a week than he did in two or three seasons. The ratio of goals to salary is such that if Shearer scores twenty-five in a season, each goal costs a headmaster's annual salary. Possible brain damage in footballers is not only to be found in players. Directors and managers would be a rich area for research, never mind Lancaster Gate.

While on the subject of old-fashioned football, what I cannot work out is, given the modern ball is so much easier to play with, not only less damaging to the brain but also more obedient to the foot, why so many players have poor close control and, more to the point, so few of them are unable to cross the ball accurately? In the England set-up, David Beckham is the exception to the rule. He can cross with accuracy and variety. Generally speaking the rest are pretty poor. You could break an ankle on the leather football and if you connected with the end of your boot it took the nail from your toe. And yet every team had a winger who could plop the ball on the centre-forward's head like a raindrop. Matthews, Finney, John Kelly were masters at floating the ball on to the brow of some rampaging forward. It would hang there for so long the only word to describe it was ripe.

What is different now is the way players can bend the ball. The leather job tended to go in a straight line although there were one or two who could make it dip. I would give anything to see the masters of my youth with the modern ball. What would Wilf Mannion, Tommy Harmer, or the wittiest of the lot, Len Shackleton, do with it? What tunes would they play? In his prime, Shackleton could take the lace out while beating his man. Nowadays he would likely make the ball disappear.

I wrote of him recently recalling the chapter in his autobiography entitled 'The Average Football Director's Knowledge of Football'. This was followed by a blank page. It caused a sensation at the time and has been much quoted ever since. A couple of readers have provided a fascinating insight into how this came about. Bill Pocock worked for Shackleton's publishers. They were certain when they read the manuscript that he had forgotten a page. Being a fan and knowing his man, Mr Pocock was able to persuade them otherwise. He had just seen Shackleton score a goal against Chelsea at Stamford Bridge and celebrate by waltzing back to the centre spot, which confirmed he wasn't normal. Just to be on the safe side, his employees insisted on explaining the situation by stating at the bottom of the blank page: 'The chapter has deliberately been left blank in accordance with the author's wishes.' This is how the most famous chapter in football biography came about – the idea every football writer ever since wished he had thought of first.

October 1998

SOCCER GENIUS MOURNS
THE DEATH OF BASIC SKILLS

TOM FINNEY resides in a quiet cul-de-sac near Preston. The bungalow glows with elbow grease and the pale winter sun glints on the silver-framed photographs of loved ones. Mrs Finney had been to the optician about her glasses and was fussing with a tea tray in the kitchen. Her husband – going on seventy-two but still a strong and purposeful figure – was telling me that generally he is still in good nick except that his left leg gives him a bit of gyp now and then.

A stranger peering through the window at this vignette of suburban life would not know he was watching one of the greatest soccer players of all time talking to yet another fan masquerading as a journalist. Tom Finney wears his eminence lightly; indeed, it could be argued that he does his best to hide it. Yet there is no denying the special place he has in the hearts and minds of those fortunate enough to have seen him play.

Trying to find his house, I became lost on the outskirts of Preston. He drove to show me the way. Two cars having a conversation on a suburban street was too much for one householder who decided to investigate. When he saw Tom Finney, he almost stood to attention. Had he been wearing a hat, he would have doffed it.

That evening, sitting in a hotel lounge in Manchester,

I was engaged in conversation by a group of shrewd, hard-headed businessmen. When I mentioned I had just returned from interviewing Tom Finney, they became like teenagers seeking news of a pop idol. It might seem silly, middle-aged men reacting like this, but if you had seen Tom Finney in his pomp you would have understood the reason for our hero worship.

Stanley Matthews, George Best and Tom Finney were the best British wingers I saw play, Best and Finney the most complete attacking players. Only Best, of the moderns, could match Finney's range of talents: the ability to operate on either wing, the capacity to play in midfield and mastermind attacking strategy. They shared two other priceless assets: they loved scoring goals, and they were fearless.

Tom Finney took a lot of stick. Nowadays, his bad leg reminds him of it. He remembers his persecutors well. 'Do you recall Stan Willemse at Chelsea?' he asked. 'Took you and the ball. Tommy Docherty and Jimmy Scoular could dish it out a bit, too. You wanted shin pads on the back of your legs playing that lot. Then there was dear old Tommy Banks at Bolton. His brother, Ralph, played in that Cup final when Stan Matthews gave him a terrible time. The first time Tommy played against Stan, he said, "Tha' might have made a mug of our kid but tha'll get no change out of me." Hard man. Had a great sense of humour. You needed one when you played against him, too.'

Finney played with Tommy Banks in the England side under Walter Winterbottom. Walter was a bit posh,

Tommy salt-of-the-earth Lancashire. During the preparation for Tommy's international debut, Walter took the team-talk and paid particular attention to Banks's opponent.

'Your winger is a good player, Tommy. Two-footed, cuts inside well, likes going outside the back, too. He's quick, crosses accurately and is a good finisher. I feel you must impose yourself on him as soon as possible,' he said.

'Can I say something, Boss?' asked Tommy.

'Certainly,' Winterbottom said, not knowing what to expect.

'Well, I'd like thi' to know that this winger that'rt goin' on abart will nobbut go past me once than I'll have him up in t'air, on to t'dog track and gi' his arse a reight good grittin'. Is that what tha' wants, Mr Winterbottom?' Banks enquired.

'Er, something like that,' said Winterbottom.

Tom Finney played 76 times for England and scored 30 goals. In 565 appearances in first-class football, he scored 247 times. These statistics become even more remarkable when you consider it wasn't until he was in his mid thirties that he started playing centre-forward.

As a child, he worshipped Alex James, who lorded it at Deepdale before moving on to Arsenal. He still treasures one of the wee man's medals given to him by his widow. He joined Preston as an amateur when he was fifteen. The club offered him pro terms of £2.50 a week but he decided to complete an apprenticeship as a plumber so that if he didn't make it at soccer he would have a proper job to fall back on. Even genius has its uncertainties.

Finney wasn't the only one with doubts about his ability to make it as a professional footballer. He first played for Preston at inside-left, like his idol. One day the outside-right of the youth team was injured. Finney was instructed by Bill Scott, the trainer, to play on the right wing. Scott then uttered the immortal line, 'Don't worry, son, we're not expecting too much from you.'

It wasn't too long after that the two best-known players in the world played for Preston and Blackpool. The media exploited the rivalry between Tom Finney and Stanley Matthews for all they were worth. According to Finney, it was a fiction. 'There wasn't any rivalry. He was simply the best ball player I ever saw in British football,' he said. 'His close control was remarkable. I never saw anyone work so near an opponent. He'd literally give the defender the ball and at the last minute flick it away. They say he would have been a luxury player in the modern game. Some luxury. He would win a game for you in ten minutes' play. He would play in any company at any time and do that. They say he didn't score too many goals. Didn't want to, that's why. Preferred to lay them on for others.'

Matthews, Mortensen, Lawton, Mannion and Finney formed an England forward line to rank with the best of all time. It is some indication of the influence Finney had on the international scene that when he played his last season for his country he was in the company of the likes of Bobby Charlton and Johnny Haynes. He looks back fondly at the calibre of his team-mates but remains very clear-eyed about their appearance on the field of play.

'They had one size of shirt for everyone in the England squad,' he said. 'So if you were six foot two it strangled you and if you were my size it came down below your knees. Same with the socks. When you put them on, they reached to the top of your thighs. Then those boots. Remember? Stiff leather, up over the ankles, bulbous toe caps. Felt like diver's boots. When it rained and the shirt collected the water and the socks were soaked, we must have weighed a ton apiece. Don't know how we moved.'

For his 76 internationals Finney was paid between £20 and £50 per match. When the team travelled by train, they went second class. It was a time when footballers, even those of genius like Finney, were kept firmly in their place. Nowadays, he watches the game avidly on television and is depressed by what he sees.

'We have to get back to grass roots, be prepared to learn,' he said. 'If you watch Italian football you invariably see intelligence and skill at work. The defenders mark close and are good on the ball. We don't have players like that. Gazza, on form, is such a relief. Tremendous ability, but the rest are very predictable.

'When the Hungarians came in 1953, I was injured but I went up to Wembley to watch. Up until that point we had thought we were the best players in the world. We were beaten 6–3 and the nation was shocked. The Hungarian side were the best international team I ever saw. They did things that day that were new and wonderful. I played against them in Budapest when we lost 7–1. It was like being an apprentice all over again.

'I think that the gap is as big now as it was then. The lessons are as obvious now as then. There's too much football. It's played at too great a pace. It seems to me that players arrive on the international scene without having served an apprenticeship. It also concerns me that talents such as those Bobby Moore possessed aren't used by the FA.'

In the everlasting debate about players from one generation fitting into another, there is no one I have ever met foolish enough to doubt that Tom Finney would have slotted perfectly into the modern game. Indeed, there is a strong case to make that he would have been an even better player because his range of skills would have given him a freer role than any allowed by Preston and England during the time he played.

When he first joined Preston, he came under the wing of a tough half-back called Bill Shankly. It was the start of a friendship and mutual admiration society that was to last until Shankly's death. Bill Shankly had no doubt that Tom Finney was the greatest player who ever lived and never tired of telling people. The story goes that one day, after extolling the virtues of Kevin Keegan, one of the Liverpool team asked him if he was as good as Tom Finney. 'As things stand at the moment, Kevin is as good a player as Finney, but you have to remember that Tommy is sixty-four,' said Shankly.

Shankly believed Finney could have played in his

overcoat and still have been great. Finney smiles at the memory of the man.

'I served my apprenticeship with men like Bill. He'd been down the pits like many of them. Proper men. He would say, "This football is a simple game, Tommy," – and that's the most profound observation to be made about it.

'One of the problems with our game at the present time is that coaches talk gibberish to children, teaching them systems, denying them the joy of playing with the ball. You hear them shouting "get rid" when they should be encouraging the lad to dribble. They murder talent with organised football.'

Tom Finney is not a regretful man. He is glad he played when he did, even though, nowadays, he would likely be living and working in Italy and gaining more in one week than he did in twenty years as a player at Preston.

He nearly went to Italy in 1952 when he was offered £10,000 to sign for Palermo, wages of £130 a month plus bonuses, a villa and a car. At the time he was earning £20 a week. Preston turned the offer down. 'Tha'll play for us or tha'll play for nobody,' the chairman told him. He has a dreamy look about him when he tells the story.

As it is, he looks back modestly on a wonderful career and a fulfilling retirement. He kept the best company, playing with the likes of Mannion ('my best partner'), Lawton, Matthews, Haynes, Peter Doherty. Di Stefano was the greatest footballer he ever saw. Of the players he watched after his retirement, Best was sublime, Dalglish would have shone in any company, Alan Hansen was as good a centre-back as Neil Franklin, and he could think of no higher praise. The best goalscorer? 'Jimmy Greaves'.

When he left football, the apprenticeship he had served as a plumber made sense. It also made him quite a bit of money. Today, Tom Finney Ltd employs 120 people specialising in plumbing, central heating and electrical work. He is president of the company and goes to work most days, despite the fact that, officially, he is retired.

He is still involved with Preston North End, is a Freeman of the town and was once chairman of the local health authority, responsible for a budget of £70 million. Tom Finney is a man you can trust, not just with money but with that more precious commodity – the awesome responsibility of being a hero.

December 1993

Tom Finney was knighted in the 1998 New Year's Honours list. Sir Tom has also become president of his beloved Preston North End, attending matches regularly as they narrowly missed promotion to the Premiership in 2001.

THE GENT WHO PUT KEEPERS
IN THE BACK OF THE NET
ALONG WITH THE BALL

THE DAY AFTER war broke out in September 1939 Nat Lofthouse joined Bolton Wanderers Football Club. He is still there. He is in his seventieth year but bright-eyed and fit-looking. He looks solid as an oak, a bit gnarled maybe, but you don't have to possess a vivid imagination to see how he terrorised defenders and why he gained the title 'The Lion of Vienna' (it's a long way form Bolton to Vienna, as they say, and more of that later). He was the most English of footballers, direct, uncompromising, fearless, hard but fair. Nothing distracted him from his job, which was to fill the net with footballs, and if necessary, goalkeepers.

In the 1958 Cup final, Bolton played Manchester United. This was the United recovering after the horror of Munich, borne to the final on an engulfing wave of sympathy and emotion. Some teams had found it difficult to play against them, had felt compromised by the public's overwhelming desire that nothing but good should ever happen to what was left of the Busby Babes. Bolton and Lofthouse put paid to the dream by winning 2–0, with Lofthouse settling matters by shoulder-charging Harry Gregg into the net. So much for sentiment. There was much debate about its legality; it certainly wasn't pretty but, by God, it was effective.

That expert judge of footballers (particularly if they were born and bred in Lancashire), H. D. Davies, wrote of him, 'Some like to get their effects by stealth, others by rank piracy. Nat is in the latter class and when he opens out all his guns he is a sight to see.'

It was on 25 May 1952, playing for England against Austria in Vienna, that Lofthouse demonstrated all the virtues Davies perceived in him, to win a famous victory in such a manner that from that moment to this, whenever you mention Nat Lofthouse, people say 'The Lion of Vienna'.

What made the game so special was its billing as the championship of Europe. We were a year or more away from meeting the Hungarians at Wembley and having our world turned upside down. In 1952 we were still a great soccer nation. Finney and Matthews were two of football's acknowledged stars. The game was given another dimension by the presence of several thousand soldiers who were garrisoned in Austria.

Lofthouse won the match several minutes from the end when he took a through-ball from Tom Finney, ran half the length of the field with the Austrians in pursuit and struck the ball home before colliding with the onrushing Austrian goalkeeper and knocking himself out. The moment moved *The Times* to report: 'For anybody who has ever seen or read football, Lofthouse will always be known as The Lion of Vienna ... It was his example all through the match that brought the scores of British soldiers pouring through the crowd at the end of the game to cheer him, lion-hearted, from the field.'

We don't call people 'lion-hearted' any more. Nowadays, we say 'they've got bottle'. We don't have centre-forwards any more. We call them strikers. It is not just that the game has changed, so has our way of thinking about it, of describing it. What would the fanzine of today make of the poem written by a fan to commemorate Nat's retirement from Bolton Wanderers:

> Lofty the Lion of Vienna
> Has retired from t'football field.
> It took a medical specialist
> To make Lofthouse finally yield.
> All t'best centre-halves in t'country
> Tried their hand at stopping our Nat.
> Nearly all had to give up the struggle,
> You can blame mother nature for that.
> Like a Centurion tank was our Nathan,
> Wi' a turn of speed like a bomb.
> Many a goalie's said sadly
> 'I wonder where that came from?'

Nat Lofthouse had a laugh when I read it to him at his office at Burnden Park. He'd forgotten it, but he liked the humour. 'Typically Bolton,' he said.

The same could be said about him. He works from the office at the club helping out with sponsors' deals, linking the club with the community. As soon as he gave up playing he came back to the club for a job. They made him second-team trainer. His first task was to clean the toilets. He had scored 255 goals for Bolton, had been capped 33 times by England and scored 30 goals, and here he was working as a lavatory attendant at his old club. It re-defines loyalty. He doesn't make much of it. 'There wasn't anything else to do, so I had to muck in,' he said.

Sometimes people say that he has a cushy job nowadays and he has to smile. When he joined Bolton, he was given two white fivers as a signing-on fee. When he took them home his father, a coal bagger with the corporation, thought he had robbed a bank. The money represented a month's wages to his dad. During the war years he worked down the pit. It made him strong.

'I was lean and hard as nails. Not an ounce of fat on me,' he said. He played his first game for England against Yugoslavia in 1950 and scored twice. He felt pretty chuffed with himself. 'Head like a bucket,' he said.

He returned home and Bolton lost to Chelsea 3–1. Nat still thought he was the bees knees. As he came off the field, George Taylor, the trainer, said, 'See me 8.30 Monday morning.' Nat said, 'It's our day off, isn't it?' And Taylor said, 'It is for the rest of t'team but not for thee.'

Nat recalled, 'When I turned up he gave me the biggest dressing-down I ever had. Told me not to be so big-headed and then said something I never forgot. He said, "You can do three things. You can run, shoot and head. You couldn't trap a bag of washing. So don't get fancy. When you play for England, you've got Matthews and Finney working for you; here at Bolton, you've got

Bobbie Langton and Doug Holden. So all I want you to do in the future is run, shoot and head."

'That's all I did really. I was fit and fast. Matthews and Finney used to put it on my forehead. Then there were players like Mannion and Carter. Finney was my favourite. I played with him twenty-odd times and on eighteen occasions his was the pass that I scored from. He and George Best were the two most complete players I ever saw,' he said.

He showed me the boardroom with his England caps in the display cabinet and then led me down the tunnel on to the pitch. When he played for Bolton Wanderers with the likes of Hartle and Banks, this was the walk that would test the nerve of the bravest opposition player.

'Ay, they didn't like playing here,' said Nat Lofthouse, looking across the pitch. I inspected the track around the ground where Tommy Banks would dump his victims. 'Gi' 'em a bit of gravel rash on the arse. Let 'em know who's the boss,' said Tommy. It is reputed that his partner, Roy Hartle, would call out, 'When tha's finished kicking thy man, Tommy, chip him over here so I can have a go at him.'

Lofthouse says, 'I used to wear my shin pads on the backs of my calves with Tommy and Roy behind me. Mind you, we were all tough and there was a wonderful team spirit. If you kicked one of our team you had to kick the other ten. But I would have hated to play against Banks and Hartle. I tell people that if Roy Hartle's mother had pulled on a No. 11 shirt and run out at

Burnden Park with the opposition, he would have kicked her to death.'

Lofthouse played his last game at Burnden Park in 1960. He played inside-right and nursemaid to a sixteen-year-old boy making his debut called Francis Lee. Lee crossed, Lofthouse scored with a header. Lee embarked on a glittering career; Lofthouse started a new life cleaning toilets and polishing boots for players who weren't fit to lace his. But he wouldn't change too much of it. He thinks being a centre-forward is much harder work than it used to be.

'Defensive tactics and patterns of play make it much more difficult to score goals. They have to do much more than run, shoot and head nowadays,' he said. 'Mind you, I'd very much like a modern team to go out just one more time and play with two backs, three half-backs and five forwards. It would be very interesting to see how the other team coped.'

I ventured that this was how Tottenham had played under Ardiles and look what happened.

'Yes, but they didn't have Banks and Hartle in defence,' he said.

Nat Lofthouse and Bolton Wanderers have been together now for fifty-five years, a remarkable test of enduring fidelity at any level, but in soccer where players and clubs often show little regard for loyalty, it is nothing short of amazing. The fact is that as well as representing Bolton's past, Nat Lofthouse also stands for the future. There is much the players of today could learn from talking to him and nothing but good to be gained from such a decent and friendly man representing the club.

As I left, my taxi driver said, 'Who have you been talking to?'

'Nat Lofthouse,' I said. I bet myself he would say 'The Lion of Vienna.'

Instead, he said, 'A gentleman. Still takes the same cap size he did when he was a lad.' I can't improve on that.

February 1995

Nat Lofthouse continues to watch Bolton Wanderers in his capacity as club president and was present when they returned to the Premiership in 2001 by beating Preston in the promotion play-off final at the Millennium Stadium, Cardiff.

FORGOTTEN HERO

DENNIS VIOLLET was once seen never forgotten. He was one of those players blessed with style. He didn't run, he glided. He didn't strike the ball, he stroked it. He was as effective as he was attractive. His career statistics – 159 goals in 259 appearances for Manchester United, 59 goals in 181 games with Stoke City – suggest a striker of the highest quality. That would be right, but only partly so, because Dennis Viollet was an all-round player of intelligence as well as quality.

His partnership with Tommy Taylor – in modern parlance they were the twin strikers of the Busby Babes, although they didn't realise it – was as subtle as it was effective. Taylor was the spearhead, powerful in the air, quick over the ground; Viollet lurking in space, prospered from the confusion his team-mate created.

He was an engaging companion who bore the trauma of Munich with fortitude and no little humour. In the history of Manchester United he tends to be overlooked, engulfed by the shadows of Taylor, Byrne, Edwards, Charlton, Best and Law. And yet whenever I think back to those days, I see him clearly.

He was never the same player after Munich. He was transferred to Stoke in 1962 and found happiness and success for five seasons under the wing of the splendid Tony Waddington and alongside the incomparable Stanley Matthews. This was the great player's swan song and Viollet was his accompanist, not to mention his accomplice.

Dennis once told me that Matthews, who was in his late forties when he rejoined Stoke, was the most extraordinary 'presence' he had ever played with. He explained that Sir Stanley's reputation alone was enough to create panic among defenders.

'His name on the teamsheet guaranteed our opponents would change tactics. Often they'd have two men marking him which made my job all the easier because of the space I was allowed. I honestly believe that if during the game Stan had gone and sat in the stand he would have had a defender on either side of him,' he said.

Dennis Viollet died the other day in America. He was sixty-five and for a long time people had forgotten him, which was neglectful and remiss. By any reckoning he had his own place in the Old Trafford pantheon.

March 1999

BOGEY'S GIFT TO JOURNALISM

I WONDER how many remember the contribution made to the *Manchester Guardian* (as it was then) and the BBC's 'Sports Report' by Don Davies, or Old International as the *Guardian* insisted on disguising him. When we discuss the great sportswriters and commentators he rarely gets a mention and yet, in my view, his contribution to soccer was as important and distinctive as John Arlott's was to cricket. It is a hard claim to justify except by memory because very little of his work is available in collected form.

More than most observers, but in common with the best, Don Davies saw soccer as a vivid interplay between players and spectators. With a shrewd eye on the field of play, he also kept an ear cocked for the illuminating quote. It was he who told us of the man on the terraces at his beloved Bolton who, after watching one player trying to beat opponents and failing, said to his neighbour, 'But why doesn't he learn how to dribble? He's got nothing else to do.'

In the days of goalposts made of iron, he reported a penalty kick striking the bar with such ferocity that the frame hummed like a tuning fork for some time after. He began one report in the *Guardian*, 'Happy is said to be the family that can eat onions together. They are for the time being separate from the world and have a harmony of aspiration. So it was with the scoring of goals at Old Trafford on Saturday.' He loved the great creative players. Of Wilf Mannion he wrote, 'Mannion is Mozartian in his exquisite workmanship. His style is so graceful and so courtly that he wouldn't be out of place if he played in a lace ruffle and the peruque.'

Reporting from Maine Road about a bad day for Manchester City, he told his BBC audience: 'City's defence line are a fine statuesque lot, but what's the good of that? Albert Square is full of 'em.'

He collected eccentrics, particularly goalkeepers. It was Davies who first pointed out that it wasn't necessary for goalkeepers to have a slate loose, but it helped. He told of Iremonger, a tall and lanky goalkeeper for Notts County, who once persuaded his skipper to let him take a penalty kick. Iremonger ran the length of the field and hit the bar with such force that the ball rebounded back over his head. Iremonger set off back towards his own goal pursued by a pack of forwards and in his eagerness to kick the ball clear scored a spectacular own goal from thirty yards.

Davies was aided and abetted in his job by the nature of the game at that time. He perished in the Manchester

United air disaster but his career embraced Billy Meredith and Bryan Douglas, Dixie Dean and John Charles, Alex James and Len Shackleton. It was a time of great individual artistry, when players were given the licence to be whimsical, even eccentric.

I never met Donny Davies and yet I felt I knew him very well indeed. We overlapped for a while when I joined the *Manchester Guardian*, but I never saw him in the office. He will never know how much I admired him and how much he fuelled my young ambition.

My problem was that I couldn't make up my mind to do either one thing or the other, which is to say play the sport or write it. For a time I tried both. As a sixteen-year-old reporter on a local paper and centre-forward for a local team, I was in the unique position to write about my own performance. I didn't exactly sell myself short. Very soon headlines like 'Parkinson on the goal trail again' became commonplace.

Even when I didn't figure on the scoresheet I made sure the report reflected the part I played in the game, thus: 'Ace goalscorer Mike Parkinson took an afternoon off from hitting the back of the net last week but was the brains behind his team's 6–0 win . . .' Any stranger I saw on the touchline automatically became a scout from a league club in the following week's paper. 'Three scouts, believed to be from Barnsley, Wolverhampton Wanderers and Manchester United, were at the game, keeping a close eye on goalscoring hot-shot Mike Parkinson . . .'

Eventually, intrigued by reports of them being where

they had never thought of going, the real scouts started turning up. At one game there were representatives from every league club in the north of England come to see this young centre-forward, who, if you believed what the local paper said about him, was at least as good as Nat Lofthouse.

They left at half-time and never came back, but even this had little effect upon fantasy. I wrote that 'offers are expected with the next few days for free-scoring Mike Parkinson from representatives of several league clubs who were greatly impressed by the young centre-forward . . .' I would have continued undeterred had it not been for the fact that in addition to reporting the doings of my own team, I had, alas, to collect results from the entire area to phone through to the Sunday papers. This involved me leaping on my cycle at the end of a game and hurtling around the local clubs. I had about an hour from the end of the game to cycle twelve miles around the local teams and phone the results through. I might not have been able to play like Nat Lofthouse but I soon had legs like him.

The problem of transferring the fantasy from professional soccer player to ace journalist was mainly one

of wardrobe. I have always been one for a uniform and what was needed to transform me was a change of costume. I was much influenced in my idea of what journalists wore by watching too many Humphrey Bogart movies in which he always dressed in snap-brim trilby and belted raincoat. I bought both. The raincoat wasn't a problem but the trilby was. There weren't too many snap-brimmed pearl-grey trilbys to be found at gents outfitters in Barnsley then. There was not much call for them. When eventually I found one, the larger problem became the question of how to keep it on my head. It was all very well for Mr Bogart but he never had to cycle around South Yorkshire in a force nine gale in his trilby hat.

Eventually I patented a chinstrap from a length of black knicker elastic and became not simply the only person in all the South Yorkshire coalfield to own a pearl-grey snap-brimmed trilby, but the only person on the planet who attached it to his head with a chinstrap made from material which normally held up ladies' drawers.

Ludicrous though I must have looked. I was too cocooned in fantasy to know or care what others thought. I was quite literally brought down to earth pedalling downhill into a stiff wind in search of results when the trilby flew from my head and acted like an arresting parachute on a returning space shuttle.

You could argue that the incident became a metaphor for my entire life. What I do know is that it was a perfect demonstration of the difference between man's aspiration and his achievement and that the trick of keeping sane is never to forget how risible we really are.

If Don Davies had one gift it was that he kept reminding us of the fact. The wonderful aspect of having heroes is not that we ever match their achievements – that is not the point. The important part is that so long as we have them, we spend time in the best possible company.

September 1991

KING OF PEOPLE'S GAME

There is fame and then there is the 'Who do you think you are?' kind which is only bestowed on the truly great, as in, 'Who do you think you are, Stirling Moss?' or 'Who do you think you are, Lester Piggott?' Anyone indulging in fancy footwork, whether returning from the pub or weaving down the wing, begged the automatic question, 'Who do you think you are, Stanley Matthews?'

You were taken to see him play as a treat. He wasn't so much a footballer as Father Christmas or a visit to the seaside. Wherever he went they closed the gates. He was the first great superstar of football and its enduring example.

I first saw him at the end of the forties. Barnsley drew Blackpool in the Cup. It was Barnsley's first all-ticket game. There were 38,000 at Oakwell to see Stanley Matthews. Put another way, there were 38,000 spectators hoping that Matthews didn't make a monkey of our left-back Gordon Pallister.

Gordon was a tall, elegant footballer, but not sprightly. He had the turning circle of an aircraft carrier. If Matthews got past him, he would have taken a week to position himself for a tackle. He owned a temperance bar in Barnsley where we would dally with a dandelion and burdock in the hope of seeing him. He did more business than usual the week of the big match. The man who opposed Stanley Matthews attracted the kind of grisly interest that attended people who faced Billy the Kid. Defenders who tried to stop Stanley Matthews were often changed by the experience. Nowadays they would be offered counselling.

As it was, Pallister played Matthews expertly. When the great man hovered on the ball inviting, nay begging, the challenge, Pallister stood off, his body angled between Matthews and the goalmouth, endeavouring to funnel him down the touchline to the corner flag. All else become secondary to this contest. It was as if the game was being played in another town until the ball arrived at Matthews' feet. In the sixtieth minute, Matthews went past Pallister for the first and only time, slid the ball to Stan Mortensen and the game was decided in that moment, as he knew it would be and prayed it wouldn't.

It was agreed that Gordon Pallister had played Matthews with intelligence and style. He was rewarded with a warm handshake after the final whistle, which didn't always happen if Matthews thought the man marking him had tried to clog him. Those were the days when such niceties mattered.

It might have been different had Matthews been playing on the left wing, which was guarded by Skinner Normanton. As it was, my hero had his hands full trying to deal with Walter Rickett, another who could dribble a bit in the days before the verb disappeared from the language.

Indeed, the Blackpool team of those days was

Stanley Matthews

crammed with fine players. Similarly, the England team had four or five huge stars reduced to the status of bit players in the presence of Matthews.

I next saw him at Hillsborough when sixty or seventy thousand people paid to see him. He was marked by Norman Curtis, a full-back with the technique and temperament of a pit bull. He was never in danger of getting a handshake from Stanley. The tactic used by Sheffield Wednesday was for Curtis to follow Matthews wherever he went. At one point Matthews went behind the goal and Curtis followed. Matthews started physical jerks and invited the full-back to do the same. Had he gone to the loo he would have found Curtis in the next stall.

I was reminded of the way defenders tried to stay close much later when Matthews made his comeback at Stoke City. He was in his forties when he went back to the Potteries, but the legend was undimmed. Dennis Viollet said his reputation made him a joy to play with because the opposition would always put two defenders on Matthews, thus leaving space for team-mates to frolic.

Tom Finney said that only George Best could be mentioned in the same breath as Stanley Matthews. I think when judged not simply as a footballer but as a man who came to represent a vanished time, Stanley Matthews stands alone. It is important not to glamorise footballers of Matthews' generation. They were exploited by managers and directors who treated them like serfs. They attracted the largest crowds in the history

of the game and were rewarded with crumbs. A triumphant end to a great career was a sweetshop or newsagents'. They had much in common with those who paid to see them. They travelled on the same buses, worked at the same pit, shared a common experience. In those days, football was the People's Game and Matthews was its monarch.

Things have changed, from the players' viewpoint much of it for the better. It is right and proper that in a game awash with money the people who put bums on seats should be rewarded. Stanley Matthews agreed with that. He knew his worth, but he was never in a position to realise it.

What has also changed is that it is impossible to imagine any modern footballer being sanctified fifty years hence, like Matthews. It is not that players of his quality are rare, simply that football is no longer a game; more a conflict.

The ultimate tragedy of modern football is that it took the death of a man who hasn't played for more than thirty years to remind us of a time when sportsmanship, courtesy, manners, good humour were not dead words but precepts without which no game is worth playing or watching. Stanley Matthews' career was a celebration of the game when it was beautiful; his death, a reminder of how ugly it has become.

I hope FIFA took note of how England supporters behaved during the playing of the Argentinian national anthem. The booing and the general abuse – now a much-loved Wembley ritual – will no doubt have convinced them that we would be hospitable and welcoming hosts of a future World Cup. The expression on Gabriel Batistuta's face told it all. It was a mixture of pity and contempt.

If the malcontents who comprise a sizeable rump of England's supporters knew anything about the game they would have saved their bile for what followed. It was a sloppy, careless game, which Argentina will want to forget. On the other hand, given our habit of clutching at straws, it has been hailed in some quarters as a significant step in the process of building an England team capable of winning Euro 2000, not to mention the World Cup.

It was an improvement on recent England performances at Wembley but that's not saying much. A lot has been made of Heskey's power and speed. He has both in abundance. What he lacks is the instinct of a goalscorer. He is a bit like a tracker dog without a sense of smell. He runs around a lot without doing the job he's paid to do.

He is young. He might learn. Dennis Wise never will. The praise for this performance ignored the fact he was booked in a friendly. Mr Keegan's gamble must be that Wise can control himself when the stakes are higher than a kick-around, when referees will be on red alert and opponents eager to exploit his, shall we say, unpredictable nature. I am glad the coach is betting with his money and not mine.

The only significance of England v. Argentina, Wembley, 23 February 2000, was that it took place on the

day Sir Stanley Matthews died and the spectators couldn't even manage a minute's uninterrupted silence in his honour.

It is not the game he loved and that's for sure.

February 2000

JOHN CHARLES WAS THE BEST CENTRE-HALF IN THE WORLD AS WELL AS THE BEST CENTRE-FORWARD

JOHN CHARLES has been poorly so I'm off to Leeds for a dinner in his honour. It promises to be a good do. Special. Like the man himself. We neglect our heroes but perhaps John Charles suffered more than most. Partly it's because he spent half his career in Italy at a time when British football was much more insular than now. In those days, playing abroad was the equivalent of disappearing down a large black hole. Also, Charles was Welsh. Had he been a rugby player, he'd have been as revered as Cliff Morgan and the rest. As it was, he retired to Cardiff and was largely forgotten.

Most of all, Charles is neglected because football is careless with the past. It always has been, but more so nowadays. The day big money swamped the game was the start of Year Zero. What went before was wiped out, which is a pity because only by understanding football's history, and particularly the players who made it special, will the game wise up.

Am I imagining it or do I spend more time these days having to explain not only what my heroes look like but what they did for a living? There was a time when every moviegoer knew Esther Williams was a swimmer and a pin-up and every football fan that John Charles was the best centre-half in the world as well as the best centre-forward. Now a question based on the aforementioned facts might cause a contestant on that quiz show to phone a friend.

For those of you who never saw him play, let me tell you what made John Charles the most talented dual-purpose player in the history of the game. He was a majestic-looking man; tall, broad-shouldered and strong. He stood two inches over 6ft, weighed 14 stone and was not to be messed with. He was light, almost dainty on his feet, beautifully balanced and quick over the ground. As a centre-forward he was a certain finisher with a powerful shot in both feet and there has never been a better header of the ball. At the heart of the defence he was unequalled.

That ought to be enough, but there is more. He had impeccable manners both on and off the field. In a career spanning fifteen years he was never booked, never sent off. The cheats and the hard men were treated with disdain. He set his own example. Playing for Juventus against Torino, he accidentally flattened the opposing centre-half as he closed in on goal. One-to-one with the

John Charles

keeper, Charles kicked the ball into touch and went to aid his fallen opponent. Even in those days it was a remarkable act of sportsmanship. Nowadays he would be bollocked by his manager, derided by the fans and lampooned by the media for doing such a silly thing. Who says the game is better now than then?

He scored 157 goals in 327 matches. That would be a remarkable effort from an out-and-out striker. It becomes all the more extraordinary when you consider that in many of those games he played at centre-half. If Emile Heskey is an £11 million player and Sol Campbell the same give or take a million or two, what would Charles be worth? You can phone a friend. Don't give me that guff about it being a different game. Charles's gifts as a footballer and an athlete would make him outstanding in any era.

Those are some of the reasons we'll be gathering in Leeds tonight to salute a player whose all-round versatility was equalled only by George Best and whose reputation as a sportsman and role model is comparable to that of Stanley Matthews, Tom Finney and Bobby Charlton.

There are other reasons, too. I shall never forget night twenty-five years ago when I was in a nightclub in Stoke-on-Trent, for charitable purposes, you understand. I was at the bar when someone tapped me on the shoulder. I turned around and this big man said gently, 'You don't know me, but my name is John Charles.'

In a sense, that introduction could well be the title of his autobiography for it sums up both the nature of the man and his fate. It is not simply unfair that heroes like Charles are forgotten, it is also wasteful. Like Bobby Charlton, he is a perfect ambassador. He should be used as an example for young players. They might not have his talent, but his respect for football and its courtesies are easily learned.

Wishful thinking. Football hurtles into space and those of us who grew up watching Charles can only watch the afterglow. Never mind. I saw him play and they didn't. I watched him at Elland Road against our record goalscorer Cec McCormack. Cec was in the middle of what the *Green 'Un* called 'a goal-scoring spree'. He was a tiny man who, even with a long stud in his boots, reached only the badge on John Charles's Leeds shirt. He had one kick that day and he scored. Barnsley drew 2–2. The Leeds manager was Major Buckley, a man who once severely reprimanded a player who failed to acknowledge him with a 'Good morning'. The same manager was so pleased when Charles scored his first hat-trick, he gave him three gallons of petrol, not realising the player did not own a car.

But what pleased us most about drawing at Elland Road was that Buckley was rumoured to be giving his players extract of monkey gland to boost their physical and mental powers. This is only to be expected from a manager who had his players dancing to music on the training pitch to improve their balance. It might not seem untoward nowadays, but in the fifties, men wearing shorts and dancing together in a field was a distinctly dodgy proposition.

All things considered, we came away from Elland Road thinking our share of the points was as much a triumph of common sense over mullarkey as anything else. Moreover, any result in a game when John Charles was part of the opposing team was reasoned to be a triumph of eleven men against twelve. Worth celebrating. That night I went to the movies and watched Esther Williams in glorious Technicolor. I made that bit up. But I could have done. In those days, it was not unusual to see a giant and a mermaid on the same day.

March 2000

A GOOD DO FOR
JOHN CHARLES

IT WAS a good do for John Charles. Lots of drink and
laughter. Nostalgia leaking from every orifice. Bobby
Collins, Peter Lorimer, Paul Reaney, Harold Williams,
Len Browning, Roy Clark, Cliff Jones, Jack Charlton
and a few others recalling the glory days with Wales and
Leeds. Peter Ridsdale, the Leeds chairman, was there to
pay his respects, but sadly neither players nor management from the present team turned up. Maybe they had
more urgent engagements. Possibly they had never heard
of John Charles. Certainly their absence was palpable,
and regrettable.

Not that Charles was making a fuss. He has the great
capacity to enjoy life no mater how daunting the prog-
nosis. For all his buffeting by illness and circumstance,
he remains a formidable presence – not as nimble as he
once was, but still straight as a pylon and strong as a
bull. Before the celebrations started, we yarned about
his life in Italy and his relationship with Omar Sivori,
the Argentinian player whom Charles rates as the best
forward he ever played with.

'He was a right ugly little bugger, so ugly that
when he scored we didn't kiss him, we ran to the other
side of the pitch,' he said. Charles and Sivori scored
250 goals between them in five seasons with Juventus.
They made a film together, became friendly with

Sophia Loren, then a Juve fan, and lived the *dolce vita*.

Sivori became involved with the Mafia. He was sharing a room with John when there was a knock on the door. Two men took Sivori outside for a talk. When the player returned he told John he was injured and couldn't play. Then he admitted he had been told he would be murdered if he scored in the next game.

Sivori did in fact turn out, but the players found it difficult to concentrate as they constantly scanned the stands for a marksman. They tried to ignore Sivori, but the Argentinian's genius for getting into trouble created a situation where a ball crossed into the opposition's penalty area, struck him on the back of the head and flew into the net. According to Charles, Sivori's team-mates formed a shield around him and smuggled him to the tunnel. He didn't wait for the end of the match but flew home to Turin. The other team equalised and then John Charles darted through the defence to score the winning goal, or so he thought. The referee blew his whistle and shouted 'offside'. The decision was so ludicrous that Charles, who never queried the ref's decision, asked him what was going on. The referee smiled and said, 'Like Mr Sivori, I too want to get home safely.'

Jack Charlton, in typically robust mood, dispelled the myth of the gentle giant. 'John ran with his arms and elbows high. When he went on a surge he would leave a terrible trail of human devastation behind him. Bloody gentle giant indeed. I once questioned an instruction he gave me on the field and in the dressing room he had me pinned against the wall and told me he'd give me a bloody hammering next time,' Charlton said.

There were other tales, too. Cliff Jones, who looks fitter than most of the present Spurs squad, particularly Darren Anderton, told a lovely story about John's mother going to watch her son when Wales played England. Mrs Charles was not a football fan and this was her first international. Sadly, her son scored an own goal but not knowing the difference, Mrs Charles was on her feet cheering her beloved as the ball flashed past his own keeper. Looking around, she wondered why she was the only person in Ninian Park celebrating her lad's genius.

It was one of those nights when sport cast its spell and grown men were soppy with fellowship and nostalgia. It was one of those nights when we saw the unique relationship that develops between an athlete and his public providing he never betrays their trust, never lets them down. John Charles fulfilled his part of the bargain, which is why he was overwhelmed with love and respect. A pity the modern Leeds players weren't present to see what happens to a real hero.

April 2000

John Charles was made a CBE in the Queen's Birthday Honours in the summer of 2001. Despite being dogged by ill health he continued to follow Leeds United from his seat in the West Stand.

SIXTIES
NOSTALGIA

ENGLAND'S IMMORTALITY
PASSES THE
TWENTY-FIVE YEAR TEST

A REPORTER rang the other day to ask what I was doing when England won the World Cup. I told him I was watching television like the rest of the country. He didn't seem happy with the answer, as if expecting me to admit I had been dancing naked around the village with garlands in my hair. He wanted to know what I had done when the Germans scored the equaliser in the last minute of the game. I told him I wasn't worried, that my money had been on our chaps all along. The truth is that I didn't see it because my eyes were closed. More than that, I was in the bathroom at the time, sitting on the loo and praying to the great Walter Winterbottom in the sky to let England win.

When I heard the roar, I rushed into the room and asked my youngest son what had happened. He said, 'Grumphgurglewillypotty,' which is what you get when you ask a two-year-old a tactical question about soccer.

I knew everything would be all right in extra time because I saw the Queen turn to Sir Stanley Rous and ask, 'What is happening?' when the players stayed on the pitch after ninety minutes. You can't fool our monarch. She knew something was up.

The reporter also wanted to know if I thought Geoff Hurst's first goal in extra time – the one he hooked in off the crossbar – was a goal. Twenty-five years on and they are still arguing about it? I told him straight. 'Fifty million Englishmen can't be wrong,' I said.

The trouble with nostalgia is it makes you feel old. It is one thing to be aware that on Tuesday it is twenty-five years since we won the World Cup. It is quite another to take your mind back all that time and place the event in the context of your own life. Only then do you realise how long ago it was and how much the world has changed.

We had just come down from Manchester and were living in a flat near St John's Wood. I was reporting soccer and cricket for a Sunday newspaper and working on a new current affairs programme on BBC television called 'Twenty-four Hours'. My colleagues in the studio were Cliff Michelmore and Kenneth Allsop.

You could say that I was playing in the First Division. Every Saturday I went to football, mainly back north because that was where Manchester United played and in those days, they were an eyeful. Best was demonstrating the upper limits of his skill. Charlton was proving that if you gave Pele equal billing, the other two greatest players in the world were both playing for Manchester United. If that wasn't enough, the imagination of Law, Charlton and Best was stoked by Paddy Crerand's diligent prompting. And you wonder why I went north each week?

Mind you, it wasn't too shabby in London. Spurs had

the likes of Alan Gilzean and Jimmy Greaves, and at Craven Cottage, Johnny Haynes was still lording it, still conducting his tutorials to a wonderful bunch of eccentrics.

To go to Craven Cottage was to laugh a lot. Most of the humour came from the disparity between Haynes's ambition and the performance of his team-mates. His relationship with Tosh Chamberlain was one of the great comic partnerships of all time. Tosh was much loved by the Fulham supporters, and quite rightly so. He was an honest toiler with a fearsome shot that brought him many spectacular goals. Haynes was supremely gifted, a magnificent distributor of the ball. The trouble between them was due to Haynes's imagination and Chamberlain's lack of it. When his plans went awry, Haynes would stand, hands on hips, looking to a distant planet to beam him up, while Tosh would untangle himself from the corner flag or the third row of spectators behind the goal.

The best bit of goalkeeping I ever saw happened at Craven Cottage and it came from a back-pass by Tosh. He was doodling with the ball on the halfway line when he decided that he would have more space if he retreated towards his own goal. There are two theories about what happened next. The first is that Tosh tried to pass back and overhit the ball, the second that he forgot which way he was facing and mistook Tony Macedo in the Fulham goal for the opposition keeper. In any event, he let rip from about forty yards. Macedo, who wasn't expecting this to happen as he assumed Tosh was on his side, flung himself to his right and tipped the ball over the bar.

That was what it was like twenty-five year ago. It was fun and a bit silly. The country was in a mess but the citizens didn't care. Mary Quant dictated the fashion, the Beatles wrote the music and Carnaby Street started in London and encircled the world.

It is important to understand what it was like in 1966 in order to comprehend how much Alf Ramsey was an alien figure in the landscape. He remains the most unlikely, incongruous icon of the 1960s. While the rest of the world went giddy, dressing like peacocks, Alf stuck to his demob suit. It was as if no one told him that the war was over. I wrote at the time that he reminded me of a puritan at an orgy.

But, while the rest of us day-dreamed about winning the World Cup in style with wingers who could dribble and the likes of Greaves lurking in the box, Alf Ramsey had a plan. It wasn't pretty, but it was certainly effective. What he searched for were individuals who might have individual weaknesses yet, when placed together, represented a unit without fault. When asked if he would pick George Best if that player had been an Englishman, Alf said he would have to think about it. He was not denying Best's genius, merely considering the possibility that in spite of all his gifts, he might not fit the jigsaw.

Looking back at what I wrote at the time, I realise I could not have been more wrong about Ramsey and what he was trying to do. But I was not the only one. Soccer managers of today who think they are misunder-

stood by the media should refer back to the kind of press Ramsey used to get and think themselves blessed. The mutual antipathy was inevitable when you consider Alf's dislike of the spotlight and our inability to understand what he was doing.

Importantly, the players felt differently about the boss. I made a film called *The Boys of '66* on the twentieth anniversary of the victory and found a unanimous and heartfelt admiration for Ramsey from all his players. He convinced them they were going to win the World Cup. 'Don't worry about Brazil,' he said when the rest of us had made them favourites.

'Pretty amazing conclusion when you think about it,' George Cohen told me, still smiling at the cast-iron certainty of his manager. Cohen said if you played for Ramsey he made you feel part of an élite outfit. On the other hand, you could never find comfort in the thought that the manager regarded you as irreplaceable. Gordon Banks, by common consent the greatest goalkeeper in the world at the time, said that after one game he bade farewell to the manager by saying, 'I'll see you.' The boss replied, 'Will you?'

Bobby Charlton tells a story about being approached by the team to sort out a problem with Ramsey. They were going to play in a hot climate and the specially tailored grey suits for the trip were made of a heavy material. Working on the principle that Charlton was the one player who could query Ramsey without getting an earful, the players delegated him to voice their complaint. Bobby told Ramsey of the problem, concluding,

'So the lads thought maybe you could let us wear our blazer and flannels rather than the suit.' Alf thought a moment and replied, 'I have a completely open mind on the matter . . . Tell them to wear the suits.'

Alf and his team won the World Cup and became the most famous men in Britain. Bobby Moore got a gong and Alf was knighted. Not too long after, Sir Alf got the sack and Bobby Moore was managing Southend United. Whichever way you look at it, we are careless with our sporting heroes.

I saw Alan Ball the other day. He has a bar and restaurant near where I live. He was saying that the players were given £1,000 each minus tax for winning the World Cup while the Football Association paid more than £1 million in tax from the profits they made. Like the rest of them, he is not bitter, more bemused by it all. For all his seventy-odd caps, he is still known as the kid who ran the legs off the Germans in extra time, part of the team who won the World Cup. The rest is measured out in anniversaries when people remember again what happened that July day in 1966.

What is missing after all these years is Alf Ramsey's account of events. Typically, he has said very little. He remained constant throughout success and failure, which is to say he revealed nothing of his true feelings. The nearest he came to verbosity was on the twentieth anniversary when he told an interviewer, 'The facts speak for themselves.'

We were filming Bobby Charlton coaching a group of youngsters and he was telling them about winning

the World Cup and how wonderful it was to understand you were the best in the world. Their eyes were as large and bright as polished hub caps. Then one said, 'Please sir, my grandad used to watch you play when he was little.' I don't know if it got to Bobby but it sure made me feel old. Mind you, he and the rest of the team have something over the rest of us. We were famous for fifteen minutes. They are immortal.

July 1991

BANKING ON MEN WITH SWAGGER AND SWANK TO INSPIRE AN UNREAL WORLD

FURTHER PROOF that the people who are in charge of the new Premier League don't live in the real world came with the announcement that the chairman of a bank will head up the organisation. This was seen by the organisers as something of a coup, whereas in the snug of the Rat and Handbag the lads were saying that a bank manager was the last person they would choose to represent either popular support or credibility.

On the other hand, if the Premier League is to be the cock-up it promises, then who better to be in charge than someone from an industry that thought the late owner of Oxford United was a man you could lend money to.

But the biggest problem soccer faces, much more difficult than the number of teams in the new League, or the quality of grounds, is how to produce the footballers to justify the revolution. What will be needed more than ever, are stars; players who can fill stadiums and restore some confidence and pride to our game. What's required is a bit of swank and swagger. I am not advocating loud-mouthed immodesty, but the kind of justifiable confidence that would lead to Sir Garfield Sobers looking out of his window early in the morning and saying, 'I'd hate to have to bowl at me today.'

You'd know what I mean if ever you saw Best and Law strut the field when United were in their pomp, or Souness lord it when Liverpool were winning everything in sight. It's what Strachan gave to Leeds and Robson to United. But it's a rare commodity nowadays. From what I've seen, modern teams lack conductors, players who dictate the rhythm and tempo of the play. The average soccer match today starts at 100 m.p.h. and only slows down through exhaustion. It has the athletic ambition and spectator appeal of a hamster on a treadmill. If that had been the soccer of my youth, I would never have bothered with the game, dismissing it for its lack of variety, imagination and above all, beauty. It was the playmakers of my youth – the Shackletons, the Carters, the Mannions, the Hayneses – who whetted the appetite and demonstrated the infinite possibilities.

They were what used to be called inside-forwards. They were always a cut above the rest. To start with they seemed more intelligent than their team-mates. They carried with them an air of intellectual superiority, sometimes even allowing themselves slight eccentricity of style – shirts outside shorts in the Corinthian (slightly foppish?) manner, hair much longer than was deemed necessary or indeed manly in those days.

We had one at Barnsley called Roy Cooling, blond and handsome. In those days I was much affected by American writers. I wrote that Cooling looked like a Scott Fitzgerald. It came out in the paper that he resembled Scott of the Antarctic. When I asked my boss for an explanation he said no one in Barnsley had heard of Scott Fitzgerald but everyone knew who the other Scott was.

Visiting inside-forwards were to be feared as much as enjoyed. They were the ones who could do terrible things to your team while making you wish you could enjoy them every week.

I watched Len Shackleton four or five times only, but I can see him clearly now against the hazy background of a thousand forgotten players and games. He was one of the greatest entertainers our game has ever produced. He illuminated the dark, drab days of post-war Britain. He gave the vast crowds who came to see him something to remember and dream about. When modern techniques of ball control are debated as if they are something new, I remember Shackleton more than forty years ago taking the ball from any angle, at any speed and taming it in an instant. His control was so sudden and subtle that you didn't realise what he was doing. He didn't trap a ball, he hypnotised it.

If he was the Cavalier of those times, Raich Carter was the Roundhead. Carter didn't run out of the tunnel on to the pitch, he would arrive in his own time at his own pace like a judge opening the local Assizes. He looked magisterial, his hair slicked down and precisely parted, his tread measured and authoritative. I first saw him play for Sunderland at Barnsley. He walked on to the pitch some time after his team-mates, looked around the field with a great show of disdain, and then meandered through the game until he decided it was time to put an end to proceedings.

He was thirty yards from our goal with his back to it when he took a wild waist-high pass on his right instep, killed it, flicked it to the ground, spun and without looking up, hit a left-foot shot into the top corner of our net. He didn't pause to see where the ball went. He knew. He continued his full turn and walked to the centre spot. That night he went into my world team to play Mars and I composed a special prayer that Mr Carter might marry a Barnsley girl and come and play for us. As it was, he ended up at Hull City where he took all the free kicks, corners, penalties and throw-ins as part of his weekly demonstration that any team with Raich Carter in it didn't need anyone else to get a result.

A bit of that is what is needed now. We require someone to put the foot on the ball and have a look around. Any scheme for the future of soccer must take into account the quality of the product. At present it's not very good, and it's significant that the discussions so far about the game's future have involved directors of clubs but not players. Perhaps the FA are working on the theory that directors are the ones who count.

December 1991

WORKING-CLASS HERO WHO WAS LIKE A KING AMONG COMMONERS

THE OBITUARIES were the sort reserved for monarchs. Those who knew and loved him would not have settled for less. He, looking down from the pantheon, would be surprised and slightly bashful. Bobby Moore knew how good a player he was, although he never boasted about it. What he never fully understood – and neither did a lot of people until he died – was the deep affection the British public felt for him.

He faced fame toe to toe and stared the impostor down. He might have been a superstar, a genuine working-class hero and a shy man, but he confronted public scrutiny with the honest and clear gaze of a man who is not easily frightened. For all his celebrity he moved easily at street level, dealing with the genuine and the crackpot in the same even-tempered manner.

When he was told that he was dying he was just as calm and unflinching. Even those who knew and thought perhaps he might want to offload his concern found him the same unperturbed, affable man, always eager to deflect questions with a cascade of enquiries of his own.

'All right, Mike?' he'd say. 'Mary OK? Boys all right? What you up to nowadays? What about the telly? Mary working? Seen Tarby? How's the golf?' By the time you had finished telling him your problems, you had forgotten what you were going to ask him in the first place. He had the most wonderful bedside manner. If there was an inner anxiety, a turmoil (and God knows there must have been at various times in his eventful life), he never let on.

It was the same with his football. His detachment from the hurly-burly was disdainful; he always looked like a king among commoners. Then when there came a champion worthy of his attention, like Pele, we saw proof, if ever it was needed, that he was one of the greatest footballers of all time.

Nowadays, when very average footballers are being sold for millions of pounds, it is interesting to speculate what Bobby Moore would be worth. At a time when players like Gascoigne, who are allegedly role models, behave outrageously and yet are still pursued by sponsors and media (who ought to know better) eager to stuff their pockets with notes, what riches would await a man like Bobby Moore, who not only looked and played like a hero, but behaved like one? The captain of the next England team to win the World Cup will drive home in a platinum Rolls-Royce, over a silver drawbridge, across a moat of liquid gold. But I doubt he will be a hero like Bobby Moore.

I am glad I saw him play when I did, when the England shirt was pristine and not daubed with commercial graffiti, when there was still honour in the game, style and, most of all, humour. The lasting image of that time

Bobby Moore

will always be Moore, slim as a reed, holding the trophy aloft at Wembley. It was the moment the boy from Barking became the golden icon of the sixties.

He had a wicked sense of humour and when he wanted he could be as hard as the best of them. We played together in a charity game when the opposition decided that it might be fun to kick Elton John into the nearby supermarket car park. Bobby had a word with the culprit, who stupidly decided not only to ignore his advice but to try kicking the great man. This foolish behaviour led to his early and permanent departure from the pitch, not that he knew what hit him; nor did the referee.

Before the game I had taken instruction from my captain on how I should play. 'Wide on the right, Parky, and when I get the ball you set off running the way I point,' he said. The first time he put the plan into operation he released me with a daisycutter inside the full-back and diagonally to the corner flag. It meant a gallop of fifty yards to get there and when I arrived I was too knackered to get the cross in. In the next twenty minutes Mr Moore deliberately delivered seven or eight more passes to the identical spot. By the end I was on hands and knees, hoping for a miracle, like a passing taxi.

Shamefully, I have to recount that I was finally removed from the pitch by the trainer after being ill near the corner flag. This greatly amused Mr Moore, who was also much taken by the report in the local paper, which said, 'Parkinson responded feebly to intelligent prompting by Bobby Moore.' It was meant as a barb.

In fact, I have been considering having it for my epitaph.

Writing all this, and remembering as I write, I keep recalling the time Dame Edith Evans was dying and her biographer and friend Bryan Forbes broke the news that she was seriously ill to one of his daughters. 'But she won't die, though, will she, Daddy?' the daughter said. 'Why not?' Bryan asked. 'Because she's not the type,' said his daughter. That's what I feel about Bobby Moore. All of us will have a chance to pay our respects at the memorial service. I only hope they can find a hall that's big enough.

March 1991

Haynes happy as pass master from Fulham's colourful days

F AME is a capricious mistress. There was a time when
Johnny Haynes was one of the most famous men in
Britain. In the fifties and sixties he was not only the
most complete footballer in the land but also the
captain of England, the first footballer to be paid £100
a week and the man who smiled at you from the
Brylcreem ads. He was universally admired and
around Craven Cottage, the home of Fulham Football
Club, he was worshipped. Nowadays, whenever you
mention his name, people say, 'Whatever happened to
him?'

The other day a radio station offered a bottle of champagne to any listener who knew where he was. The
curiosity was well meant and can be regarded as an
indication that he has not been forgotten.

On the other hand, any suggestion that Haynes lives
anywhere other than the pantheon is an insult to anyone
who saw him play. If you compile a list of English
players of equal calibre, only Bobby Charlton, Bobby
Moore, Tom Finney and Stanley Matthews come to
mind. Together they comprise the crown jewels of English football.

In fact, Johnny Haynes is alive and well and living in

Edinburgh. He helps his wife run a dry-cleaning business. He often delivers door to door. I wonder how many of his customers realise they are being served by a man who once masterminded the most humiliating defeat ever inflicted on the Scottish national team. It was 15 April 1961 – England 9 Scotland 3. Jimmy Greaves scored a hat-trick, but it was Haynes at his merciless best who controlled the slaughter. He also scored twice.

Frank Haffey, the Scottish goalkeeper, lived the rest of his career with the noose of that defeat around his neck. The occasion was celebrated by a bitter joke. Scottish fan to Johnny Haynes: 'What time is it?' Johnny Haynes: 'Nine past Haffey.'

He was waiting for me in the arrival lounge at Edinburgh airport. There wasn't anyone marking him. He always had the knack of finding space. The hair was greyer than I remembered, but cut in the same no-nonsense, national service style. He is sixty-one and in very good nick. As he leads the way to the car park, I look at the broad and solid back, the rolling and purposeful gait and imagine that is the view most defenders had of him when he was in his prime. Like his old friend Bobby Moore, he is genuinely self-effacing. He knows his reputation and does not see the necessity to continue proving it. He would much rather gossip about old friends back in London than his life and times.

Again like Bobby Moore, he throws you off the scent by asking questions. 'Seen Jimmy [Hill]? How is he?

All right? What about Tom [Wilson]? Remember those lunches we used to have? Good times, weren't they? Do you see anything of Bobby [Keetch]? He's a character, isn't he? How's George [Cohen]? Ever see him?' And so on until you are in danger of forgetting that he is supposed to be answering questions not asking them.

When he finished at Fulham he spent a few years coaching in South Africa. He played under his old friend 'Budgie' Byrne, whose theories on man-management were sometimes as whimsical as his manner of playing. He once asked John if he could criticise him at a team meeting so that the rest of the players, who were in awe of Haynes, would think themselves in good company when the manager took them to task.

Haynes reluctantly agreed. 'Remember,' said Budgie, knowing his friend's short fuse. 'whatever you do, don't come back. It's only pretend.' Came the day and Byrne was in the middle of dressing down Haynes when the player started answering back. What was meant as a dummy run became a full-scale slanging match as both men argued and nearly came to blows.

Haynes laughs at his inability to side-step an argument, even a make-believe one. He never did. When he was one of the most famous names in football, he managed to enjoy his celebrity without it ever dominating his life. Anyone imagining that temptation in those days was not as alluring and available as it is now never walked down King's Road in the sixties nor fully understood Fulham FC's affinity with the more glamorous, not to say raffish, elements of London society.

Honor Blackman, known in those days as Cathy Gale or Pussy Galore, had a seat in the stand and there were more showbiz faces on the terraces than would be found at the Royal Command Performance. It is rumoured that Johnny Haynes was once unable to get into the treatment room for a massage because the facilities were being used to 'prepare' a greyhound for a big race.

Tommy Trinder was the chairman and he was not the biggest comedian on Fulham's books at the time. There was the immortal Tosh Chamberlain, whom God created for Johnny Haynes to shout at. It is difficult to imagine a more contrasting pair – Haynes the perfectionist, stern and meticulous; Chamberlain, carefree, and so careless of his talents as to appear, on occasions, slapdash, not to say doolally. Anyone watching Fulham in those days is bound to remember Haynes with the ball at his feet, pointing Chamberlain down the wing. When he was in full flight, Haynes would release a thirty or forty-yard pass of such exquisite direction and pace the ball would drop like a snowflake on to Chamberlain's right to-cap. What happened next would depend upon the tide, or the state of the moon, or the juxtaposition of Mars with Venus, or from which side of the bed Tosh had alighted that morning. Sometimes he would continue his run, stride unbroken, and crash the ball into the net with a ferocity unequalled in the days of heavy leather balls.

Chamberlain once broke a goalkeeper's arm with a penalty. Playing against an Italian club, the entire defensive wall broke ranks and fled in disarray as Tosh ran in to take a free kick. Equally, he demolished a few corner flags in his time and had also been known to smash the ball into the crowd behind the goal causing the kind of devastation normally associated with a six-inch mortar.

Sometimes he would trip over himself and fall flat on his face. On these occasions he would pick himself up and come face to face with an outraged Haynes who would bawl him out. There was the famous moment when the argument became so heated that the referee booked Tosh for abusive language. 'But you can't do that, he's on my bloody side,' said Tosh.

In those wonderful, intoxicating, funny days, Fulham had a centre-half called Bobby Keetch. Anyone tracing the family tree of the modern footballer and seeking the moment when he crossed the divide between sport and showbiz – made the change from snug to cocktail bar, started going to a hair stylist instead of a barber – should talk to Mr Keetch about his time at Fulham.

Bobby Keetch drove a silver Lotus Elan sportscar, bought his suits from a Mayfair tailor, ate at the Chanterelle in South Kensington, and drank with Annigoni, the odd opera singer and one or two train robbers at the Pheasantry Club in Chelsea. He had great natural style and a compelling attraction for the opposite sex, particularly debs who had seen nothing quite like him; nor had the rest of us.

Haynes was Bobby Keetch's hero. Today the two men remain firm friends. Keetch, now a successful businessman, has little doubt that Haynes was among the best ever.

'One of the truly greats. I was seventeen when I joined Fulham. John was captain of England. First day we went to a pub for lunch and I sat apart from the others. Didn't dare speak. The team left and I asked for my bill. The landlord said that John had paid for me. Didn't have to, except he knew that as a young player I was likely to be broke and I was. It proved my theory that I never met a really great player who was a complete a*** hole,' he said. On the basis that people should reap what they sow, Keetch took Haynes and his wife to Rome to celebrate the great man's sixtieth birthday. They prevented a lot of vino from being consigned to the European wine lake.

The first time they went to Italy together was with Fulham. Haynes and Keetch were sitting in a restaurant in Venice when a beautiful woman asked Bobby Keetch if she might paint his portrait. Mr Keetch did not return with the main party. Haynes remains in awe of his friend's panache.

Keetch says, 'His great hero is Tom Finney, and I think John stands comparison. Like Finney, he has been given a retrospective accolade. It's only in recent years that people have come to realise they were both truly great players. Can you imagine a time when we were able to take footballers of that calibre for granted?

'I think John was the best passer of the ball I ever saw. His accuracy was remarkable over distance and the weight and speed of the ball was always perfect. He was the master of the long, defence-splitting pass. It's been lost to the game in recent years, but I saw Ruud Gullitt playing at Chelsea and he hit a couple of forty-yarders to feet that had men of my age remembering John.

'When people ask me about him, I tell them that he was a perfectionist and sometimes he achieved perfection. Not many of us can say that,' said Bobby Keetch.

He might have lacked ambition. Otherwise why stay at Fulham? The nearest he came to leaving was when John White, the greatly gifted Spurs inside-forward, was tragically killed. Spurs offered £100,000 for him. Today they would need five million or more. He was tempted. He thought Jimmy Greaves with his intelligence and predatory instinct in the box would have been a perfect partner. Fulham would not part with him.

The news that the club had blocked the transfer was too much for one reader who wrote to a newspaper editor: 'This strikes a deadly blow at our trade union rights and liberties. We might as well have let Hitler come over here with his jackboots and trample all over our cherished and hard-won liberties.'

Had Johnny Haynes played today he would have been a millionaire. As it was, he found financial security by going into partnership with a bookmaker called Tommy Benfield. They sold their betting shops to the Tote, and Haynes had a safety net against the moment the tumult faded.

He played 56 times for England, 22 times as captain. It would have been more but for a damaged knee caused by a car crash when he was twenty-seven. He says he played for seven years on one leg.

The argument goes that he might have had a more illustrious career, become a better player, had he gone to a bigger, wealthier club. Haynes points out that when the Fulham team included Tony Macedo, Jim Langley, George Cohen, Bobby Robson, Alan Mullery, Eddie Lowe, Archie Macauley, Bedford Jezzard, Rodney Marsh, Graham Leggatt, Allan Clarke and Roy Bentley he could claim to be in the best of company. What kept it interesting was the presence of characters such as Maurice Cook, Jimmy Hill, Tosh and Bobby Keetch. In the First Division days of the sixties, Fulham attracted gates of 40,000.

In 1961 Jimmy Hill, the man who gave professional footballers a clear and persuasive voice as well as a new deal, drove through the restrictions imposed by the maximum wage. Tommy Trinder, who once joked that Johnny Haynes was worth £100 a week, was made to put his money where his mouth was. There were those who predicted it was the beginning of the end. Haynes smiles at the memory.

'I'd love to play in today's game. I think I'd find a lot of space to put my foot on the ball and pass it around. I think I might enjoy working with the modern ball. It's difficult to explain to players just how heavy and brutal the old ball was.

'Once we played on a mud heap at Port Vale and even Tosh, who could kick a wall down, couldn't move the ball more than ten or twelve yards. Roy Bentley who played centre-forward and centre-half for us, had a forehead covered in scar tissue,' he said.

He did not fancy management. He took over on a temporary basis when Fulham sacked Bobby Robson as the team went from First to Third Division in three seasons. 'Didn't like it. I valued my health too much. I saw what it did to other people,' he said.

One day when Vic Buckingham was in charge, Haynes watched him try to teach Bobby Keetch how to become a better player. Buckingham took Keetch on to the training ground and started tap dancing. At the end of a five-minute routine borrowed from Fred Astaire, Buckingham said to a baffled Bobby Keetch, 'That's what I want you to do. Learn that routine. It'll do wonders for your balance.' 'F*** off,' said Bobby Keetch and earned himself a free transfer.

We laughed a lot that day in Edinburgh. Why not? We were remembering good days when football wore a smile. Anyone who went to Craven Cottage when Johnny Haynes was king will tell you the same. It was not a golden age or anything like that – although it has been a while since we produced a Haynes, a Charlton or a Bobby Moore – but it was a pleasant, well-mannered and good-natured time to be involved with the game.

There was nowhere else we would rather be on a Saturday afternoon than watching football at Craven Cottage. I asked Johnny Haynes what he remembered when he looked back. 'I recall that once we scored a hundred goals and didn't come top. We couldn't work it out until someone pointed out that we'd let in a hundred goals as well. It was great fun, wasn't it?' he said.

January 1996

Johnny Haynes savoured Fulham's return to the top division in 2001 from his Edinburgh home. Bobby Keetch died of a heart attack on 27 June 1996, almost exactly five months after this interview appeared.

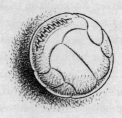

A HERO AND GOD STRICKEN
LIKE AN ORDINARY MORTAL

W HEN I HEARD that Danny Blanchflower had died
I tried to remember the last time we met. I
thought it had been at Wentworth Golf Club five or six
years ago when we talked about his days at Barnsley
and laughed a lot. It wasn't until I saw the newsreels of
him sick and infirm at his testimonial that I realised
this was the last occasion I saw him. I had deliberately
exorcised the memory. The dreadful illness that made
him frail, dimmed those marvellous eyes, muddled that
keen mind, was distressing to behold. It was also inap-
propriate. He was a hero, a god, so how could he possibly be stricken like an ordinary man?

Blanchflower illuminated my youth. He, like Tom
Finney, John Kelly and Wilf Mannion, defined for me
a game of high technical skill, graceful athleticism and
often vivid imagination. It was also played with a great
deal of humour and sportsmanship. They were the finest
role models a boy could wish for.

Blanchflower's was the most persuasive example of
all because the rest were but occasional visitors to
my youth, whereas, for two marvellous seasons,
Blanchflower was a part of it. Barnsley bought him from
Glentoran in 1949 for £6,000. He played his first game
against Rotherham United and we had to admit that
we'd seen nothing like him. What was also obvious was

that he wouldn't stay long at Barnsley; he was destined to move on to the highest levels of the game. Whenever he turned out for the Tykes it was something of a special event. Every game was a farewell. He rarely let us down. Even in his springtime he was a footballer of great technical quality and maturity.

The first thing you noticed about Blanchflower was his balance which enabled him to survive the sternest challenge and, added to his marvellous close control, gave him the luxury all great players share, that of playing in their own private space at their own tempo.

He was one of the best passers of a football I ever saw. He skimmed, stroked, chipped and curved passes all over the field with a quarterback's feel for weight and trajectory. He had a disdain for defending. It wasn't that he was a shirker or lacked physical courage, simply that he believed it was an area of the game better left to the players who enjoyed doing it.

At Barnsley, the mugging of visiting forwards was done by Danny's midfield partner, the incomparable Skinner Normanton. At Tottenham, in more illustrious company, Dave Mackay did the same job on Danny's behalf. Beauty and the Beast.

When, later on in life, I came to know Danny Blanchflower, he often talked about his days at Oakwell. He remembered that when he first arrived for training he imagined that the soccer would be more cerebral than he had played in Ireland. In his first practice game he encountered Skinner without knowing anything of his

Danny Blanchflower

reputation for what can best be described as an uncomplicated approach to soccer.

As Skinner approached Danny with the ball at his feet, Danny quickly considered all the tricks that might be employed to beat him: would Skinner give him the body swerve, would he use the feint inside, might he waggle his foot over the ball daring Blanchflower to guess which way he was going? As it was, Danny ended up flat on his back with Skinner's studmarks up his shirt front as Skinner walked through and over him. It was a suitable introduction to his new club and his midfield partner. It might have been worse because Danny told me that Skinner was once sent from the field by his manager during a practice game in which he inflicted serious damage on a team-mate

If Barnsley gave him his first taste of football in England, it also gave him a valuable insight into the way our soccer clubs treated their players in the fifties.

After training in the morning, the Barnsley players spent most afternoons playing snooker in a local hall. During a poor sequence of results, the manager received complaints from the fans that he was allowing his players too much time playing snooker when they ought to be practising football. As a gesture he summoned his players to the ground in the afternoons which meant they merely played snooker at the club instead of the snooker hall. Blanchflower asked for the ball. He was told he couldn't have one because over-familiarity with the ball would deaden his appetite for it on Saturdays. He replied, famously, that if he didn't see the ball during the week he wouldn't know what it looked like on Saturdays.

He was accused of being a trouble-maker and transferred, without much ado, to Aston Villa. He sat in the kitchen of the hotel with a cup of tea while the chairmen of the two clubs haggled over a price in the dining room. He was treated like a piece of meat and the affront lit a fire in him that burned and raged for the rest of his life.

He had a fine contempt for directors of football clubs and throughout his career never lost an opportunity to larrup them for what he considered their ignorance of the game and lack of understanding of players and managers. He was the most eloquent advocate of the beautiful game and its most passionate defender. He could talk the leg off an iron pot and, at his best, write with real style and imagination.

He lost the war against the Philistines, otherwise he would not have been such a ghostly, marginal figure in the game he adorned long before he was rendered unemployable by his ghastly illness. It was unseemly and unutterably sad that such a proud and independent man should be sustained by charity at the end of his life.

Those of us who enjoyed his company, read him, watched him play will understand the significance of Danny Blanchflower. He was an important man in the history of football. He never compromised his own vision of how the game should be played, never lost his disdain for those who couldn't tell the difference between success and glory. A lifetime in football taught him the valuable lesson that the difference between winning and losing, success and failure, is balanced on a razor's edge.

After defeat in the 1958 World Cup in Sweden, when he captained his country, he wrote: 'In the highly intensive world of professional football the sun rises and sets with alarming suddenness. The world turns over every twenty-four hours, but not with the smooth astronomical rhythm that compels our planet. It just gives a quick, impulsive spin and the character who has been basking in the summit sunshine unexpectedly finds himself clinging desperately to the South Pole with cold, bare fingers.'

With hindsight, that statement becomes an awful prophecy when applied to the last wretched years of his life. Reading the many generous obituaries about him I wondered how, for the last decade or so, the world became so neglectful of a man of such obvious quality. The sadness of it all is that often we only tell our heroes how important they are when they can no longer hear.

December 1993

COHEN JUST HAPPY TO BE
ALIVE AND JOIN THE
SURVIVORS OF '66

S IR ALF RAMSEY, not a man renowned for shooting off at the mouth, described George Cohen and Ray Wilson as the greatest pair of full-backs ever to play for England. The judgement was made in 1966 and nothing that has happened since would make him change his mind.

It might be that next Tuesday they renew their partnership at a dinner in London to celebrate the thirtieth anniversary of winning the World Cup. Nothing is definite because the dinner is an *ad hoc* affair (the Football Association seem to have forgotten the anniversary) and in any event Ray Wilson feels lost if he goes any further south than Sheffield. He lives a calm and isolated life in remote hills much like the great Wilson of the *Wizard*, existing, I have no doubt, on a diet of spring water and wild berries.

His partner is much more the city dweller. George Cohen was born in Fulham. He played for Fulham all his life. When Johnny Haynes ran the manor, he was one of his able lieutenants. As an England player, he liked attacking down the wing, giving the necessary width to Ramsey's wingless wonders, relying on his speed and stamina to get back quickly for defensive duties.

He played thirty-seven times for England and won the biggest medal of them all. He had thirteen seasons with his beloved Fulham and didn't win a sausage. He gave up football in 1969 because of injury. He was the last Fulham player to be capped by England.

Since then a lot has happened to George Cohen, some of it very unpleasant. In a week when a television programme revealed a muddled history of misdiagnosis and delay in treating Bobby Moore's fatal cancer, George Cohen had added reason for being thankful his illness was swiftly diagnosed and treated. He suffered cancer of the stomach ten years after playing in the World Cup final. He had two major operations and six years of treatment at the Royal Marsden. He says it was like living in a twilight world because he needed so many pain-killing injections.

When you meet George Cohen, it is hard to believe he was so ill he was twice given up for dead. He lives in Tunbridge Wells and when he walked into the lounge of the Spa Hotel he looked like a successful businessman who kept himself in shape. There was only the set of the shoulders and the balanced, slightly pigeon-toed walk on the balls of the feet, to indicate the athlete.

He is an intelligent, articulate man who makes a living as a property developer. During the recession, times were hard but he was unfazed. 'Worse things have happened to me,' he said.

Recently, during Euro '96, there was a revival of interest in the boys of '66. It was somehow reassuring when watching the black and white images of victory to be reminded of a time of modest heroes when commentators knew enough words to concoct a memorable phrase and only lions were rampant on the England shirt.

He thinks the players of the sixties were better technically than the current crop and certainly better disciplined. When I asked him about Ramsey, he immediately told me of the time Bobby Moore and six of the players sneaked out for a meal before a friendly international against Portugal. They returned to find their passports on the bed. The next day, Ramsey told them that had he been able to find replacements they would all have been on the plane home and would not have played again. 'When Alf said things like that, you didn't argue,' said Cohen.

When you ask him about the team, he feels he doesn't have to say much about the obvious heroes like Charlton and Moore – 'It's all been said.' He says he doesn't think Stiles or Ball get the credit they deserve. 'Stiles against Eusebio in the semi-final was one of the greatest demonstrations of marking I have ever seen. Nobby was always there. If I made a mistake, he'd be covering, if I sat on my backside, he'd be alongside collecting the ball. As for Alan Ball, I used to say he was the best winger I've ever played in front of,' he said.

He says Ramsey's gift was to bring together a group of players who fully complemented each other. 'There was no weakness in the chain, either in terms of the way we played or the way we lived together. There was a maturity about us because Alf treated us like grown men,' he said.

As Glenn Hoddle takes over, he would do well to consider the way the '66 team have represented themselves and the game in the intervening years and wonder how he might persuade his players to see the virtue of setting an example as well as winning trophies.

George Cohen never had a problem putting fame into perspective. Playing for Fulham all his life gave him a keen insight into the transient nature of things. After the World Cup everyone wanted to know him. At one garden party he was introduced to the assembly as 'George Cohen of West Ham'. Recently displaying his World Cup memorabilia at a school fête, he was approached by a child who said, 'Excuse me, sir, but is the recipient of these caps and medals still alive?'

This is gentle stuff for anyone who played at Fulham in the sixties. 'Great place, special crowd. Those standing on the Thames side of the ground used to pee into the river at half-time. Remember?' Who could forget. In the days when Jimmy Hill sporting a little pointy beard was in the side, he once made a run and screamed at George Cohen to slip him the ball in an open space. As he became more frantic in his pleadings, a wag on the terrace shouted, 'Cohen, when the Rabbi asks for the ball, let him have it.'

He thinks John Haynes the best 'foot to ball' player he ever saw. Explain. 'It simply means he was technically perfect. It didn't matter how you hit the ball to him, he was always balanced to receive and move straightaway.

To see him volley a ball was to witness perfection of technique and timing,' he said.

George Cohen was twenty-nine when a serious knee injury caused him to leave the game. He received £10,000 insurance from the club and the proceeds of a testimonial game at Fulham. He had commenced his new life away from the game when he was diagnosed as suffering from stomach cancer. Twice, his wife was told to put their effects in order. She took no notice. Why? 'She told me, "I could never see you dying,"' he said.

He went to the Royal Marsden for chemotherapy and radiotherapy. He said, 'When I was a kid growing up in Fulham, if you went to the Marsden you were a gonner. They used to have a whip round in the street for the family.'

He got better. He still has the odd bad day but has lived to see his boys grow into men and to experience the bliss of being a grandfather. He works to raise funds for a children's cancer unit at the Royal Marsden in Sutton. Next Tuesday he will meet the rest of the survivors of '66 and have a yarn.

When you say it is strange the FA seem to have ignored the anniversary, he smiles and shrugs. This is someone who has endured too much ever to be discomfited by the actions of petty and inadequate men. When you ask him what he really remembers about that July day thirty years ago, he recalls Alf Ramsey's words as they approached extra time – 'You've beaten them once, now go out and do it again.' George Cohen did not fully understand the meaning of those words on that special day. He does now.

July 1996

George Cohen was awarded the MBE in the New Year's Honours in 2000, along with four other 'forgotten' members of England's World Cup-winning team. He works for Fulham as a matchday host, as well as retaining his property business. His cancer is still in remission.

How England were made to pay by the manager who got away

Jack Charlton is a flinty man. He was hewn not born. I don't want to make him sound unfriendly because he is not, but where others more gifted have strolled down life's boulevard, he has battled every inch of the way, and it shows. He might be in his seventh decade but there is no mistaking the warning in his pale blue eyes, jutting chin, straight-backed, physical presence. The jib has a very purposeful cut to it. There is about him an impatience that gives the impression of being forever on the move.

When we met the other day he arrived in the foyer of a hotel in Reading carrying a holdall and suit looking like he was coming and going at the same time. Arranging a meeting with him requires an intimate knowledge of railway schedules up and down the land. He arrived at 12.30 p.m. from Cardiff. He was leaving on the 2.07 to Southampton. When you finally get together with Mr Charlton, even the most elaborate arrangement seems like a chance meeting. You know how Stanley felt when he encountered Dr Livingstone.

Since he left the job managing the Irish team, he has been on the move, whether it be fishing, flogging his book or making speeches. He is an engaging after-dinner speaker with the dry self-deprecating style of the best north country comedians. His classic story is about the World Cup final when England were 3–2 up and hanging on for dear life. Bobby Moore, severely pressed in his own penalty area, controlled the ball on his chest, pulled it down and played a one-two with Alan Ball. Charlton watched this with disbelief. This was not the time for fancy football but an occasion when the ball should be kicked into the stand if not out of the ground. With Charlton bellowing at Moore to get rid, the England captain looked upfield and played the perfect pass into the path of Geoff Hurst who scored the fourth goal. Jack Charlton says, 'I remember looking at my captain and thinking, "I will never be able to play this bloody game."'

He didn't think he was good enough to be an international footballer and was nearly thirty years old when Alf Ramsey proved him wrong. He once asked Sir Alf what he had in mind when he picked him to play for England. Ramsey said, 'I have a pattern of play in my mind and I pick the players I think will best fit the pattern. That doesn't necessarily mean I pick the best players, Jack.' What attracted Ramsey as much as Charlton's strength in the air and in the tackle was his unyielding character and unbending will. There have been many footballers more gifted than Charlton but few more staunch.

It could be argued that Jack Charlton and his brother, Bobby, became footballers because of genetic engineering. Four uncles and a cousin – the immortal Jackie

Milburn – played professional football. From an early age, Bobby Charlton displayed the talents that made him special in any company, but Jack Charlton didn't find it was easy. He left school at fifteen and went down the pit like his dad. He didn't like it and thought he might become a policeman when Leeds United signed him. He made 629 league appearances for the club.

The best part of Jack's autobiography is his account of growing up in a mining community, playing street football, buying his first fishing rod and taking a step down the path of lifelong addiction to angling. He shared a bed with his brothers. It wasn't until he did his national service that he slept by himself. At the centre of his life was his mother Cissie, devoted to bringing up her family, particularly Bobby, the youngest. Jack Charlton has never forgotten his background and although the game has brought him fame and riches, what he experienced growing up in Ashington still controls his nature and informs his understanding of things.

The saddest part of the book is his account of growing apart from his brother. Bobby Charlton never had a more loyal advocate than his brother, who thought him one of the greatest footballers there had ever been. Jack Charlton grew up looking after 'our kid', understanding without pique that his brother was his mother's favourite. It continued into adulthood. Whenever Leeds played Manchester United she would tell Jack, 'Now don't you go kicking our Robert today.' It says something for Jack Charlton's love of family that he never did, although there was an occasion when his brother nutmegged him and Jack chased him towards goal shouting, 'Don't even think about scoring.'

Ironically, the rift in their relationship was about their mother. As Jack Charlton tells it, his brother grew apart from the family causing deep upset. I asked him why he felt he had to make family business public. 'The public already knew about it,' he said. 'I really didn't want to revive it in the book but I was persuaded that because it was public knowledge it would seem strange if I didn't refer to it. I read it ten times or more and changed it every time. It was difficult and done more in sorrow than in anger. Because we're brothers doesn't mean we're the same person.'

It is not in Jack Charlton's nature to be diplomatic. His approach to life is very direct, sometimes on the brutal side of straightforward. Only the Football Association were shocked and surprised when he famously confessed to an interviewer that he kept a 'little black book' to remind him of opponents he intended to get even with. It wasn't meant to be taken literally but it caused a terrible stink at the time. Anyone who had ever played against Jack Charlton was not the slightest bit surprised. They knew that any misdemeanour against his person would be paid back in kind even though it might take a while. Johnny Morrissey, an aggressive winger with Everton, went through a Charlton tackle and caused the defender to have his foot in plaster. As he left the ground, Morrissey said, 'How's the foot, big fella?' and grinned. Charlton said, 'If it takes me ten f****** years I'll get you back.' And he did. 'In fact,

Jack Charlton

we kicked each other at every opportunity until we finished playing,' said Jack.

Charlton remembers the encounters with something like affection. Referees were also aware of what might happen if he was fouled. George Kirby, of Southampton, was a tough centre-forward who dished it out. One encounter flattened Charlton. When he got to his feet he was groggy. The referee came up to him. 'Give it five minutes, Jack,' he said. 'For what?' said Jack, puzzled. 'Before you try to get your own back,' said the referee.

He was as uncompromising as a manager. He had two gifted teachers, Don Revie and Alf Ramsey. Revie taught him about the importance of attention to detail; Ramsey showed him how to pick the right player for a specific role. When he became manager of the Republic of Ireland team, he proved he had been an attentive pupil, transforming a hopeless cause into a glorious enterprise. When the whole team met the Pope prior to the World Cup finals of 1990, his Holiness John Paul II said to Cissie Charlton's lad, 'I know who you are, you're the boss.'

Charlton's affair with Irish football was too passionate and intense to have a happy ending. He informed the authorities that if Ireland didn't qualify for the European Championship he would resign. He was told not to be hasty, which is what he wanted to hear. He wanted to choose the moment and the manner of his leaving.

Within two days he was summoned to Dublin and sat opposite the four men from the Football Association of Ireland with whom he had shared the revival. Never one to shilly-shally he asked them if they wanted him to go. No one replied. So Jack Charlton pointed at them individually and asked them again. They all nodded. The way he tells it, it would make a great scene in a movie. He says, 'It was sad it had to end that way because we had been through a lot together. But what hasn't changed is the attitude of the Irish supporters. They gave me the best time of my life and I shall be forever grateful.'

His success with Ireland again begged the question of what he might have achieved had he been appointed manager of England. He applied in 1977, the only time he applied for a job in his life. He didn't even receive an acknowledgement for his letter. He doesn't know why he was so rudely treated although as student of the workings of the Football Association he can't have been too surprised. His revenge was achieved by proxy. When he was appointed manager of Ireland, Sir Bert Millichip, Chairman on the FA said to Des Casey, president of the FAI, 'You made a mistake appointing that man.' When Ireland beat England in Stuttgart in 1988 and drew with them at Wembley in 1991, Casey said to Millichip, 'Quite a good mistake we made, wasn't it?'

What now for Jack Charlton? He is too restless to spend the rest of his days fishing. He says, 'I don't know about the future. Maybe I don't want to be a total football man again.' On the other hand, I sense the right offer might tempt him back. Will it come, or is there perhaps a perception that this uncompromising proponent of simple, direct football would be lost in the political maze of today's game? He doesn't see a problem. 'Football hasn't changed since I first played it in the street. We've complicated it by playing in a way that suits our opponents in the rest of the world.'

The more football becomes a trendy part of our popular culture, more showbiz than sport, the more it forgets its roots, the more important it becomes for people like Jack Charlton to be around to remind us of the game's cradle.

October 1996

Jack Charlton did not return to football management but remained a forceful and thoughtful commentator on the sport through his media work and as an in-demand after-dinner speaker.

OF BEST, BACCHUS
AND BUSBY

THE LAST TIME Manchester United played in a final of the European Cup, in 1968, I was bored stiff for most of the game. Manchester United were lucky it went to extra time because Eusebio should have scored with three minutes left. Alex Stepney's reflex save was astonishing, but a player of Eusebio's calibre should have buried the chance.

In the opening minutes of extra time, Stepney cleared the ball downfield, Kidd flicked it on and George Best stuck it through the centre-half's legs. Now he was one on one with the goalkeeper – a foregone conclusion. George dummied, the goalkeeper fell for it, and United were ahead. From that moment on, Benfica crumbled and Matt Busby fulfilled his final ambition.

George Best remembers the game but little else. There was a reception, a banquet and a trip to a nightclub, but he has no recollection of the part he played in the celebrations. His friends tell him he had the meal but afterwards nipped off to spend the night with a girl-friend. Looking back, he thinks it might have been the moment when his life went into freefall, when Bacchus replaced Busby. Three decades and several lifetimes later, Best has been forced to confront his memories by a media and a public gorged with the game, pigged out on a mixture of frenzy and hyperbole.

He treads diplomatically around the debate about whether or not he played in a better team than Ryan Giggs. It is at least debatable, whereas the other question, who was the better player, Best or Giggs, is not. Indeed, none of the players on view in the European Cup final will come anywhere near possessing Best's remarkable range of skills.

Dr Frankenstein might produce a decent replica if he combined the best of Beckham, Keane, Giggs and Yorke, plus Teddy Sheringham's forehead. Even then it would fall someway short of the real thing. It is difficult explaining to people who didn't see him play how different George Best was. It is near impossible to convince young people who have known just the portly and frayed imposter of recent years that this was once not only a great footballer but also a man as glamorous as any film star.

I would give anything to see Best playing in the Premier League. It is the perfect theatre for him to cast his spell. Beckham on the right, Best on the left – now that would be something to make even cynics drool.

When considering the qualities of players like Best, who operated at the sharp end, you have to remember the sixties was the time when forwards were not a protected species. In fact, it was open season for defenders, who were given *carte blanche* to kick opponents. British football in those days was no place for players of a nervous disposition. The faint-hearted had nowhere to hide. At Highbury, Peter Storey awaited, at Chelsea, 'Chopper' Harris clattered all comers, Tommy Smith bossed Anfield and at Elland Road, if Norman Hunter didn't get you then there was a fair chance Billy Bremner would, and there was always Jack Charlton.

Best had his card marked in his very first game. It was against West Bromwich Albion at Old Trafford and he was opposed by a feisty full-back called Graham Williams, who spent most of the first half trying to persuade George he was in the wrong job. Best in those days had the physique of a knitting needle but he took Williams on, even daring to nutmeg him, which was the equivalent of signing his own death warrant. In the second half, Busby switched Best to the other wing, thus ensuring that his career lasted one more game. Ever after, when Williams met Best, he would ask him to stand still so he could study his face. 'I want to know what you look like because all I've ever seen of you is your arse disappearing down the touchline,' he said.

Best survived, prospered and triumphed because he was supremely gifted and could overcome any challenge, be it physical, mental or tactical. Like all the great players, the foundation of his talent was his balance. His low-slung way of running allowed him to ride the roughest passage if he was equipped with stabilisers. His speed often took him away from trouble before it could hinder him and his stamina ensured that he was still operating flat-out when the opposition became heavy-legged. Those qualities were God-given, but what he built on that foundation sets an example today's footballers might take to heart.

He made himself into a two-footed player, not in the

George Best

sense that he was marvellous with one and adequate with the other, but to the point where he had forgotten which was his natural foot. This gave him all the option when it came to beating the opponent but particularly in the box, where Best was one of the most certain finishers I ever saw.

It is interesting to note that Bobby Charlton was another Manchester United player of the time who was completely two-footed. None of the current crop of forwards are. You might think that with upwards of £25,000 a week coming in, they would bother to learn.

Best was the complete player, the most naturally gifted Busby ever saw. When he was at his most sublime, he was unstoppable and irresistible. After a virtuoso performance against Chelsea at Stamford Bridge, the crowd stood and applauded him off the field. His love of showboating often led to frustration among team members who would spend the afternoon running into support positions, only to watch Best being indulgent.

In training, he kept the ball for so long they introduced two-touch football. Two touches and you gave the ball away. Best took one touch, then played the ball against the shins of an opponent, taking the return and setting himself up for another two. So they introduced one-touch football. Again, he played the first touch against a team-mate's legs, took the rebound and, like a pinball wizard, cannoned his way through defence to goal.

When he bought his first house, he invited a gang of friends to see Manchester United play Newcastle before going on to the house-warming party. The game was a fairly dull affair with George keeping out of trouble until he received a throw from the keeper and ran to the touchline below the spot where his guests were sitting.

He gave us a wave and then stood foot on ball, awaiting the arrival of the Newcastle United defence. Three of them approached and just when it seemed they had him cornered, he flicked three wall passes off their legs, chipped over their heads, collected the ball and then turned and gave us a bow. In those days, he was a man in love with his virtuosity, certain of his ability because he had taken nothing for granted.

George Best did not arrive on earth the complete player. He made himself into a truly exceptional footballer by working hard and intelligently at the game, which makes his downfall even more of a mystery.

I don't know why he chose to drink himself into oblivion; nor, I suspect, does he. It is for sure he could have been better looked after when he arrived at Manchester United, particularly when it became obvious he was as much a pop star as a footballer.

He was the first player to step into showbiz. That was the problem. The present crop take their lifestyles and their acclaim for granted. They are represented (more often than not, misrepresented) by agents and managers. They are protected by bodyguards and, in the case of Giggs, a stern and watchful manager. Best lived in digs with Mrs Fullaway, parked his Jaguar in the road outside and had ten sacks of unanswered fan letters in his bedroom. No one bothered because no one knew what was happening to him and by the time they cottoned on, it was too late.

At first, he was having a lovely time. The football was magical, and the sixties were a perfect time to be single, good-looking and horny. Sometimes, when he wanted a change of scene or to escape the media, he would come and stay. He spent most of the time in the garden playing with my sons. One of them was asked by their teacher to tell the class what he had done over the weekend. 'Please, Miss,' he said, 'yesterday I played football with George Best.' She gave him a dressing-down for telling fibs.

One night, he went out to a nightclub and next morning at breakfast asked if I could take him to London. Mary was making herself a cup of coffee when down the stairs from George's bedroom walked a pretty young woman wearing evening dress and smoking a Balkan Sobranie. George had brought her home from his night out but had omitted to inform us. She was a nice girl and offered to do the washing-up. Mary thought she might ruin her dress so the girl, determined to impress, started tottering around the house in high heels doing the Hoovering.

I have been a friend of George Best for nearly forty years and it has never been dull. On the other hand, I suspect that his friends – or most of them I know – had a better time than George did. There is within him a profound melancholy, not altogether attributable to Celtic gloom.

Best thinks the real trip downhill started after his

team won the European Cup, in which case the coming week will be a poignant occasion in more ways than one. His life has been turned into a feature film and it will be interesting to see if they manage to pin him down. I doubt it. Even before booze took a grip on his personality, he was a contradictory and elusive character. They have an even bigger challenge when they try to depict what he did on the field of play. Finney, Maradona or Pele would be the only adequate substitutes.

If Best has no regrets, it would be presumptuous of those lucky enough to have watched him and know him to feel cheated. Yet the fact remains he left the game aged twenty-seven, before he reached his prime. We don't know what might have been. The real tragedy of George Best is neither does he.

May 1999

George Best continued to wrestle with alcoholism and had implants inserted into his stomach in a bid to conquer his addiction early in 2001. He also worked for SkySports as a studio summariser of live football.

A NEW CHAPTER IN THE LIFE OF BRIAN AS A BRIGHTER FUTURE COMES INTO FOCUS

W HEN I told people I had been to see Brian Clough, the first thing they wanted to know was how he looked. They had heard the tales of him being found legless in charge of a football club, listened to the rumours that he had become an alcoholic recluse, looked at recent photographs and reached their own conclusions.

All I can tell you is that when I met him he didn't look like a pisspot to me, and I have met a few in a far from sheltered career. On the other hand, it would be misleading to pretend there had never been a problem and that he wasn't involved in a running battle to prevent booze dominating his life. I asked him how bad it had been.

'I was in an environment where people drank. We drank after the match with the opposition. That was social drinking. Then we'd drink to celebrate if we won and drink to drown our sorrows if we lost. That way it becomes a habit. I am not making an excuse, merely stating a simple fact. Also, I was in an occupation where rumours abound. One day I was doing and interview with a journalist and his phone went. After taking the call he said, "That was my wife. She's just heard on the news that you're dead."

'Well, reports of my death were greatly exaggerated. Similarly, so were reports of my drinking. Tom Jones once said to me that if he had knocked off all the birds he was rumoured to have done, he would never have had the time to sing a song, or the energy. Same with me and drink. If I had drunk every bottle of whisky or seen off every bottle of champagne I was supposed to have supped, you and I wouldn't be here right now laughing about it,' he said.

In his autobiography, he says, 'There have been times when I allowed my drinking to take a hold . . . Whatever steps are necessary to set my friends and family at ease, I will take them. No one is going to be able to brand Brian Clough as a drinker who lost control and could not conquer his habit. I will beat it.'

When I met him he said he was off the booze. He was gearing up for a nationwide tour to promote the book and had spent the morning signing copies in his publisher's warehouse. When he gives his press conference on Monday and then spends the next three weeks meeting the public, it will be a significant and intriguing return to public life and being under scrutiny. Given Brian Clough's penchant for making waves, it is unlikely to be without incident.

Already he finds himself embroiled in a controversy because of a chapter in the book in which he states that he believes the Liverpool fans who died in the Hillsborough tragedy were killed by Liverpool people. I asked him why he felt it necessary to publish his opinion.

'Because I was there. [Nottingham Forest were to play

Liverpool that day.] It would have been cowardly not to say what I saw and what I felt. Nonetheless, it did cause me heartache and agony deciding what to say. I must admit that had they printed everything I said I think I might have been hung, drawn and quartered. My son plays for Liverpool. He is walking down the same street as people who went through that awful tragedy. So I have to be careful.

'But I was there and I can't forget what I saw. First of all, before two o'clock I saw the fans all looking smart and happy with their Liverpool rosettes, poking their noses through the fences. But before that, I saw the other element spewing out of the pubs. Not a shadow of doubt that many of them didn't have tickets. These were the ones who caused the trouble. I have no doubt that the police did make mistakes, but when a tragedy such as Hillsborough occurs, several things are to blame,' he said.

I asked him if he had received any hostile reaction to his views. 'Not at all. The most reaction has been from people who said, "We all know what happened but we didn't say it."'

It is not in Clough's nature to be circumspect. He is impatient, dogmatic, arrogant and confrontational. His wife says that during his life he has lurched from crisis to crisis, that he didn't mature until late in life. He himself says that he was boastful and achieved 'pinnacles of rudeness'. On the other hand, he has been married to Barbara for thirty-five years, his children are well brought up and loving, and every Sunday there is a

Brian Clough

family get-together, so he is not all ogre. He must have done something right.

Professionally, there is little doubt that he was one of the greatest managers the game has produced; or that he was the best manager England never had. Although those who played for him might tremble at his approach and live in fear of his wrath, few would deny that working with Clough was a unique and unmissable experience. Martin O'Neill, who played under Clough at Nottingham, said, 'I've seen big men hide in corridors to avoid him. He was egocentric, sometimes a bully, often impossible. But I wouldn't have missed a moment of it because, in the end, as a manager he was magical.' This was after O'Neill had read the book, in which Clough had written that he was a good player but 'a pain in the arse'. Some would use stronger language in assessment of Clough. There are those who dismiss him as a loudmouthed prat, while others place him as a manager alongside Shankly, Busby and Stein and as a human-being regard him as a significant working-class hero.

Both schools of thought will find comfort in the auto-biography. In that sense, the book is honest, because reading it is like meeting him: it is a rip-roaring adventure with Clough, broadsword in hand, cleaving his way through life. If it as if Flashman had made football his career. What it doesn't give you is any real insight or explanation of the man and his job. Clough is not one for navel gazing. For someone whose greatest skill was in discovering gifts in players they didn't know they possessed, he is remarkably shy about putting his own hidden depths on display. 'I'm a bighead not a figurehead,' is the nearest he gets to self-analysis.

What is difficult to portray in print is Clough's warmth and sense of humour, at best displayed when he starts listening to himself then spontaneously erupts at what he has heard himself say. I will give you an example.

We were talking about the modern game and I asked what he thought about it. He said, 'The game has changed. Referees are in danger of becoming over-zealous in applying the letter of the law. They need to get the balance right. Mind you, some good has come of it. We are allowing players to play who were once too frightened to walk down the tunnel because they knew they were going to get a clattering. Today they come down like King Kong. They run all over the place thinking, "No bugger can kick me now." Not a bad thing.'

So far so good from a man who practised what he preached by producing teams more concerned with playing football than kicking opponents. But there was more, and this is where it went a bit off the rails.

'Mind you, I think it would be wrong to deny the physical part of our game. It is part of our culture to play hard. Like roast beef and Yorkshire pudding, fish and chips. Fish and chip are good for you. All right, let's take a chip . . .' He held up an imaginary chip in his fingers and looked at it admiringly. 'Lots of vitamins in a chip. Nothing wrong with a good old English chip.

If you go on the bloody Continent they eat frogs' legs and all that. Nobody tells them to stop eating frogs' legs. You don't hear them cribbing about frogs' legs.' By this time we were both looking at the imaginary frogs' leg that had replaced the chip in his fingers. Our eyes met and he started laughing at the lunacy of it all. 'Silly bugger,' he said to himself.

The most evocative part of the book is his account of growing up in Middlesbrough. He was one of eight children. It was, he says, a blissfully happy childhood. He was useless at school and not much good when he sought an apprenticeship as a fitter and turner. He settled for a motto: ignorance is bliss. Then he found football.

'Someone told me I was good at it. Then I found the confidence to believe I could play football. Next I was able to look at other kids and say, "I'm better than him." It gave me a yardstick in life,' he said.

Did he find football fulfilling? I asked because he was never a subscriber to Shankly's theory that it was more important than life or death. When he was a manager, he insisted his young players go to college for an education, he went on holiday with his family in the middle of the season, and opened the turnstiles at Nottingham to striking miners as a declaration of his support.

'Yes, I've been fulfilled. Put it this way, I've had most of what the game's had to offer,' he said.

When people talk of Brian Clough they often forget the fact that he was out of the ordinary as a player, never mind a manager. Playing for Middlesbrough and

Sunderland, he scored 267 goals in 296 appearances. He can safely claim his record will not be broken. He was only twenty-six and an England international when an injury to his knee forced him to retire. The rest, as they say, is history.

His first managerial job was at Hartlepool. He was joined by Peter Taylor, who was to become a major factor in his career. His book is dedicated to Taylor's memory. It says: 'Still miss you badly. You once said, "When you get shot of me there won't be much laughter in your life." You were right.'

Their first season together, Hartlepool won promotion. Next came Derby County. They were a Second Division side when Clough joined them, First Division champions when he left. Brighton and Leeds followed, both short stays and, in the case of Leeds, farcically brief.

Clough became manager of Nottingham Forest in 1975. Two years later they were promoted from the Second Division; the next season they won the First Division and the League Cup. They secured the League Cup three more times, won the European Cup twice and, in the eighteen years he was in charge, were only out of the top ten on two occasions, the last when Forest were relegated and Clough announced his retirement.

His mentors in management were Alan Brown and Harry Storer. Brown, who managed Sunderland when Clough played there, taught him discipline and the importance of good behaviour.

'He detested shabby appearance, unkempt hair. I always insisted that my players looked smart. He wouldn't stand for any nonsense on the field, no arguing with the referee. Nor would I. He made an immense impression on me. Most of all, he taught me that a football club manager is the boss. You can have your chairman, chief executive and the rest. They are nothing, nobodies unless the manager gets it right.'

But what about the extra ingredient, that Svengali-like quality that enabled Clough to bring the best out of players who had hitherto been discarded by other good judges as being either troublesome, ordinary or over the top? John McGovern, John Robertson, Kenny Burns, Larry Lloyd, Dave Mackay, John O'Hare and Alan Hinton are just a few examples of footballers given a new life by the judgement of Clough and Peter Taylor. Clough offers a few clues.

'Coaching is for kids. If a player can't trap a ball and pass it by the time he's in the team, he shouldn't be there in the first place. I told Roy McFarland to go and get his bloody hair cut – that's coaching at top level,' he said.

In the week before playing Hamburg in the final of the European Cup, with the German team planning tactics in a training camp, Clough took his players to Majorca.

'We did bugger all for a week. The Germans were rehearsing corner kicks and set pieces. We were busy doing nothing.' Nottingham Forest beat Hamburg 1–0 and won the European Cup for the second time.

Harry Storer, who managed Birmingham and Derby County, was another whose advice Clough sought and acted upon. Storer told him, 'When you become a manager and you are leaving for an away game, look around the team coach and count the number of hearts. If you are lucky there will be five. If there aren't, turn the coach round and go back.' Clough said, 'I took his advice when appointing my captains – Mackay, McFarland, John McGovern, Stuart Pearce – all courageous men who led by example.'

In his last, unhappy season with Nottingham Forest, he had cause to remember another Storer observation. Talking about directors of football clubs, Storer told him, 'Don't ever forget, directors never say thank you.' When Clough retired from Nottingham Forest after eighteen seasons, he received a silver rose bowl – 'very nice' – but not one of the directors wrote to him. 'One or two of their wives did but not the directors themselves. Strange, isn't it?' he said.

A sadness he has had to bear is that his judgement finally betrayed him when it came to deciding the moment of his leaving. He should have retired after Nottingham Forest lost to Spurs in the '91 Cup final. He didn't, and suffered the ignominy of leaving the club in the season it was relegated.

More than that, there had been allegations of shady dealings in Cup final tickets and reports that his work at the club had been undermined by his drinking, that he had sometimes been seen 'legless' before lunchtime. It would not have been typical had he gone quietly, but this was neither the closing ceremony he anticipated nor, more to the point, deserved. When I ask him about it he is, for the first time, lost for words. He grimaces and shakes his head. 'It should have been different,' is what he finally managed. But he is not complaining. He is too bold and positive by nature to be a whinger.

Looking back, he has few regrets. He had an opportunity to stand for Parliament when Labour offered him the chance to oppose Winston Churchill in Moss Side. He was told they had visions of making him Minister for Sport. He decided to stay in football and wonders now what kind of a Member of Parliament he might have made. 'Not a good one,' according to Kenneth Clarke, a Nottingham Forest fan. 'He hasn't got the patience to be an MP. What's more, he doesn't debate, he argues.' I passed on the observation to Clough. 'He's quite right,' he said. 'If I went into the House, I'd want to be the Speaker.'

He is still a member of the Labour Party, still gets involved in the odd cause. He was once heckled by a man who wanted to know how he could be a socialist and drive a big car. He thinks back to his childhood and mourns the lack of opportunity suffered by his parents and their generation.

'We were allowed to fulfil our ambitions, they were not. My mother was in her sixties before she flew. I sent her off in a helicopter one day to fly to the Channel Isles. When I saw her she said, "Is that flying?" I said it was and she said to me, "I don't want to travel any other way from now on." That's nice, isn't it?' he said.

And how is Clough taking to retirement? 'No bullshit, it is beautiful, should have done it long ago. The biggest question you have to ask yourself when you wake up is, "Is it Tuesday?" It's a lovely relaxing feeling. I hardly give soccer a thought. I have been to two matches to watch Nigel play at Liverpool but I haven't been to see Forest play. The last thing Frank Clark wants is to see me striding through the gates. He's doing well, Frank, and it might be that after Christmas I will see a bit more football. As it is, I work in the garden and teach my grandchildren how to cheat at dominoes. They might as well learn straightaway that life is not always bathed in sunshine.'

It will be interesting to see what happens to Brian Clough as he tours the country promoting his book. His patience might be stretched if the questioning concentrates on the state of his health as much as on his achievements as a manager. All he need remember is that in the final analysis, he will be judged as a football man and that being the case, only a dolt would deny him a place in the pantheon.

One final question, Brian. In the book, you say that you keep your mother's mangle in the front room at home. On top is the cask bearing the scroll declaring you a Freeman of the City of Nottingham. Why?

'Well, to remind me where I came from to where I arrived. When I was a kid I used to mangle the sheets for my mam. It's a symbol,' he said. I said I understood its significance, but wasn't a mangle a curious object to have in your front room? He gave me the Brian Clough glare, chin tilted as if inviting a punch. 'Listen to me,' he said, forefinger jabbing the air. 'If Prince Charles can take a bloody teddy bear to bed, what's wrong with me having a mangle in my front room?'

As another football fan with a sense of humour was fond of saying, 'There's no answer to that.'

November 1994

Brian Clough had a stand named after him at Nottingham Forest. On the rare occasions he attended matches, it was to watch Burton Albion, the Southern League club where his son Nigel became player-manager.

THE MODERN
GAME

PASSION IS A SUBSTITUTE
WORD FOR SKILL

THERE is a school of thought that says the sooner Paul Gascoigne takes himself off to America the better. There is another that argues America is not far enough away.

If our last view of him turns out to be that of a podgy, out-of-condition footballer blubbering at his own foolishness, it's a fair picture of what he has become in the last years. Any sympathy we might feel for a fellow human being crying out in pain and frustration is quickly tempered by the realisation that the hurt was self-inflicted and that in the past his victims have included more vulnerable targets than George Boateng. The statement from Mel Stein, Gascoigne's manager, that Boateng's chin must be made of rock, serves only to illuminate the Gormenghast world occupied by Gascoigne and his acolytes.

As a lawyer, Mr Stein must know that had Gascoigne's elbow come into contact with a citizen's face in a shopping precinct or, more likely, in a nightclub and the event been caught on CCTV, his client might be investigated by an organisation much less sympathetic than the Football Association; and he might possibly spend time in an institution with fewer creature comforts than The Priory – not as cosy, but cheaper.

If and when Gascoigne leaves these shores it would

be wonderful if he took a few other players with him. Who would miss Dennis Wise, Roy Keane, Lee Bowyer, Frank Leboeuf, Stan Collymore or that much-decorated football ambassador Ian Wright, whose move to Burnley proclaims an ambition to get a red card in every division? They are not the only ones, simply the best known of the Premier League footballers who do so much to make the game they play as beautiful and appealing as a septic tank.

It is tempting to suggest one way of restoring the game's reputation would be a summit involving players, referees, managers, directors and the game's governing bodies. They had something like that only recently and all that came out of it was the present anarchy.

At the centre of this mess are the referees. If that much-abused phrase 'lack of consistency' has any place at all in the present situation, it is when applied to the conflicting instructions given to match officials. One minute they are expected to behave like Vlad the Impaler, the next, Larry the Lamb.

In the final analysis, referees have little to do with transforming the game. Only the players can do that. It is their choice. Either they learn to accept the referee's decision uncomplainingly, or the game deteriorates into the kind of disagreeable spectacle seen on a regular basis in the Premier League.

Of course, managers must play their part (there's a laugh), directors too (there's a bigger laugh) and the FA must ensure the highest standards of behaviour from all concerned (stop it or I'll wee myself laughing).

Paul Gascoigne

The game is in its present state because all the above parties conspired to make it ugly and confrontational. It is said that it was ever thus and our present concerns mere echoes of the past. I've watched football for more than fifty years and in all that time I have never witnessed the game so adrift from its roots, so at odds with those established sporting traditions of fair play – owning up, accepting the referee's decision and, most of all, taking responsibility for one's actions and facing the consequences without whingeing or bursting into tears.

Gascoigne's waterworks should be set to music and used as an example of the state English soccer had reached at the turn of the century. His decline over the past decade is a paradigm of the game's problems. The drunkenness, the violence, both on and off the field, the disregard of authority, the denial of responsibility as a role model, the mawkish self-pity are as symptomatic of English football as a whole as they are aspects of Gascoigne's persona.

Similarly, just as the player's downfall was as much a result of feeble management at every level as it was due to any defect in his personality, so football in England was assisted to its present state by agents who are either witless or cynical or both, managers who often sacrifice their principles to protect stars and an executive, whether it be in the boardroom or at national level, who like the Duke of Plaza Toro has set the example by leading from the rear.

Examples abound. In spite of all the evidence to the

contrary, Ian Wright told reporters that children were not influenced by players' behaviour. He said, 'The kids respect me for what I am.' Dear God, I hope not. This is a man whom the FA in its infinite wisdom made an ambassador of the game and who was awarded a gong by a grateful government. It may be that Wright is a hero to kids *because* of his confrontations with authority and his flaunting of sporting decency. If that's the case then the entire game – and I don't just mean football – is well and truly up.

What about those pathetic footballers from Leicester who were kicked out of their hotel after Stan Collymore set off a fire extinguisher? Collymore was given community service. What had any community done to deserve him?

Most revealingly at all, the Leicester hooligans were not punished as severely as they might have been because there had been a mistake about their curfew time. The manager wanted them tucked up with their rusks by midnight. They thought they merely had to be back at the hotel at that time and, provided they were, could go on getting more and more plastered until they fell down or someone set off a fire extinguisher, whichever came first.

Have you ever heard such pathetic tripe? Grown men, highly paid athletes, having to be told when to go to bed? What kind of woeful, gormless poltroons are they who have to be wet-nursed and nannied like small children?

Kevin Keegan gave the clearest possible signal to serial

offenders that they are welcome in the England squad by picking Dennis Wise, who, even if he gets away with the present charge against him of bringing the game into disrepute, has proven time and time again that given a choice between being sensible or stupid he will always opt for the early bath.

Mr Keegan talked of players like Wise having 'passion'. It's the game's buzzword at present. It's a substitute word for skill. What it means is when faced with players of superior technique give them a good kicking. It is what England coaches have to resort to because we are inadequate when compared to the teams who really compete in World Cups and don't just make up the numbers like us (if we are lucky).

If our players spent as much time working on their imperfections as they do drinking, they might understand that in reality 'passion' is no substitute for quality. It is a word from the vocabulary of desperate men.

The immaturity and arrested development of our footballers stem from a laddish culture sadly not confined to football, but it does find its most fertile ground in a game where there is a ton of money and a mite of intelligence. How often do we hear players and managers talking about 'the lads', as if describing callow, unrazored youth? Dennis Wise is thirty-four, Ian Wright is thirty-six, Roy Keane is twenty-eight and Stan Collymore twenty-nine. Grown men? Certainly. Mature adults? I ask you.

Nor are the media blameless. Too often they are the lickspittles of football not its scrutineers. By employing some of the game's dubious characters they promote doublespeak and chicanery. They glamorise the meretricious when they should be exposing it.

I haven't yet mentioned the racism that still exists on the terraces, the foul abuse that is the chorus against which every game is set or the violence on the streets. These problems are shoved under the carpet when we are bidding for a World Cup, not to mention an Olympic Games – which brings us to the Wembley fiasco and the link 'twixt politicians and football. But that, dear reader, is another can of worms

Football is a big mess. It is a multi-million pound industry involving third-rate people. There is no easy fix because the biggest problem the game has is that the players, who can change it most of all by restoring decent behaviour and standards to the field of play, still believe referees are to blame. That is how dim they are and how lost the cause.

PASSING THE BLAME DURING OUR HARD WINTER OF DISCONTENT

ROAD TO NOWHERE
The story of English football 1990–93
A tragedy in three acts

ACT I

Scene: Lancaster Gate, headquarters of the Football Association. Outside a gang of English football supporters have gathered to protest about England not qualifying for the World Cup. Some are carrying machetes; one or two have their coats over their heads. They are in an angry mood. They are chanting:

Chorus of yobs:
> What are we going to do for the next three years?
> Who are we going to find to crunch?
> No more fisticuffs with foreign queers
> No more Krauts or Frogs to punch.
> We are the lads of the bovver brigades,
> We've done the biz from Rome to Mytholmroyd.
> We've sorted out the Kikes, the Wops and superspades,
> And now we find we're effing unemployed.

Inside the building, the FA are in a crisis meeting. Some members are slumped in their chairs. Their average age is

86½. The chairman Bert Megachump, 97, turns from the window.

MEGACHUMP: What's wrong with that lot out there?

KELLY: (Megachump's butler): They're blaming us for not going to America.

MEGACHUMP: Have you issued a statement?

KELLY: Yes. I've blamed truancy in our schools, single parent families, VAT on heating, video games, amusement arcades, drugs and the media.

MEGACHUMP: Well done.

There are cheers from the assembled committee and cries of 'bravo' from those members still awake.

ALBERT SHIRT (89, chairman of the Brighouse and Rastrick Brass Band FC): What my lads want to know is what we are going to do about it?

KELLY: As is well known, the official policy of the FA in times of crisis is to do nothing.

SWALES (an expert in management): Sack Taylor. Appoint a new manager.

EPHRAIM TWERP (103, retired ironmonger and chairman of Back Wallop FC): Bring back Walter Winterbottom. And what about Alf Ramsey?

SWALES (suddenly excited): Ramsey. That's a great idea. Won a World Cup, nearly won another. What happened to him?

KELLY: We sacked him.

MEGACHUMP: We must advertise the post. Normal sort of thing. 'Manager required for England football team. No professional footballers or foreigners need apply. Knowledge of football desirable but not obligatory.' I only want the ad in the papers that haven't said nasty things about us in recent years.

KELLY: Which are those, Boss?

MEGACHUMP: *News Chronicle, Daily Sketch, Reynolds News* and *Daily Herald.*

KELLY: Good thinking, guv.

MEGACHUMP: Now let us discuss the really important business, which is the trip of the official FA party to the World Cup. We've hired an air ambulance to take the committee. We won't alter our plans because we didn't qualify. If the team's not good enough, that's their bloody silly fault.

Cries of 'hear, hear' and 'bravo' and 'mine's a large gin and tonic' are heard through the windows by the fans outside who are listening to a recording of Luciano Pavarotti singing the England World Cup anthem, 'The Donkey Serenade'.

ACT II

Scene: An FA coaching course at Lilleshall. A large picture of Charles Hughes, the director of coaching, dominates the room. Underneath the portrait is the famous aphorism by Horace: *Dolce et decorum est, ludere longo folle.* Translated, this means: 'It is a sweet and seemly thing to play the long-ball game.' Speaking is Persimmon Prat, chairman of the Public

Schools FA and author of *From Agrippa to Graham Taylor: Coaching Through the Ages.*

PRAT: There has been much ill-informed criticism of our leader, Charles Hughes, following events in Bologna. His critics say he relies too much on the long-ball philosophy and that his coaches are not professional footballers but teachers, and too academic. Nonsense. As Aristotle famously said, 'Plato is dear to me but dearer still is truth.' We are here to teach you the fundamentals of the English game based on a flat back-four, known to FA coaches as *quarta acies posterior.* Similarly, we like to call the long-ball game *ludere longo folle*, so as to avoid any confusion. Also, we recommend that if you are pleased with your team's performance, you remember the Latin phrase *pueri bene bonum fecerunt*, which roughly translated means, 'The lads done well, good.'

I would now like to introduce you to the man responsible for the state of the game in England today, the man without whom there would not have been the triumph against San Marino. Our leader, Charles Hughes.

Hughes is taken to the platform on a throne carried by four FA coaches wearing blazers festooned with badges. A choir of one thousand junior soccer players sing, 'Long ball, long ball' to the tune 'Amazing Grace' as the procession moves through the cheering throng.

HUGHES: Let me explain our philosophy. We invented the long ball to miss out the midfield because it was no use passing to players who couldn't control the ball. What we didn't realise until it was too late was that our front men couldn't control the ball either.

Therefore I have amended the FA coaching manual. In

future, we will miss out our attacking players as well and shoot at goal instead. We must therefore produce players who can shoot from inside their own half. This is the new direct route. We have three years to practise before we conquer the world.

Remember the motto of the Football Association: *Stulti videmur non sumus*. Roughly translated, this means: 'We are not as daft as we look.'

He is carried in triumph to his waiting helicopter. Outside the hall, a group of ex-England international football players who have been excluded from the course stand in mute respect. They carry a banner bearing the legend: WE ARE AS SICK AS A PARROTUS.

ACT III

Graham Taylor stands centre stage, illuminated by a single spotlight. An orchestra starts playing 'My Way'. Taylor begins to sing:

> And now the end is near,
> I've had my chips, I must be going.
> I've shed a little tear,
> Said my farewells,
> The press are crowing.
> We've failed to qualify,
> We stuffed it up along the highway.
> I can't escape the fact,
> We did it my way.
>
> Regrets? I've had a lot,
> But one or two I'd like to mention.
> I'd like to keep the job

Until I get a proper pension.
I took a lot of stick,
Was called a turnip and a carrot.
No wonder I was choked,
Sick as a parrot.

What good is a man, though an absolute charmer,
If he chooses a player like Carlton Palmer?
What can a man do if Gazza's a dollop,
And the rest of his team a load of codswallop?
The record shows, the FA know, we did it our way.

Bugle sounds the 'Last Post'. Two men carrying a coffin marked 'English football 1993 RIP' walk sadly across the stage. Slow curtain.

November 1993

SUPREME STRIKER IS A BRIGHT LIGHT WITHOUT THE FLASH

WHEN ALAN SHEARER answers, he creases his forehead and knits his eyebrows in concentration. He has the same look when chasing a through-ball on goal. He is a trier, whether he is considering daft questions or scoring the goals that have made him one of the most valuable players in world football. This year he could have gone to Italy, filled the vaults with money and sampled *la dolce vita*. Instead, he settled for another four years at Blackburn, a pleasant enough town, but not to be compared to Rome, whichever way you look at it.

There is something attractively old-fashioned about Alan Shearer. He is a superstar but he is not flash. He manages to be a modern idol without wearing an earring, having his head shaved or saying 'wiv' instead of 'with'. He is friendly and polite and talks a lot about his wife and family, mum and dad. I am going on about the way he is because in the modern game he represents a bright light in a naughty world.

There might be those who, upon reading what I have written, will conclude that Shearer is too well-mannered to spend much time in the hurly-burly of the penalty box. They would be making a terrible mistake. He is almost recklessly brave in his pursuit of goals. He is tough, resolute, skilful. He is as good a centre-forward as I have ever seen, designed by physique and temperament to fill the net with footballs, sometimes when they are still attached to goalkeepers.

He has reinforced his natural attributes with the best advice. When he was at Southampton, he played in a practice match against that splendid veteran and eccentric keeper John Burridge. Shearer went for a throughball and when Burridge dived at his feet, jumped over the keeper's dive. Burridge told him, 'When a keeper dives at your feet, he expects a clattering. Don't disappoint him.' A couple of years later, Burridge played against Southampton when he was with Falkirk. There was a fifty-fifty ball and this time Shearer did not pull out of the challenge. Burridge needed three stitches above his eye. He said to Shearer, 'Well done.'

When I tell Shearer that he reminds me of the heroes of my youth, Nat Lofthouse, Wally Ardron, George Robledo, he understands the compliment. He wears the No. 9 on his back like they did, he is built to the same specification. He has strong lets, a big backside, wide hip. His boss, Kenny Dalglish, was built the same way, and he could play a bit. He doesn't mind sticking his head where it might get kicked.

'Scoring goals is what I'm about. It's what I'm paid to do. If that means putting my head down where the boots are flying, I'm prepared to do it,' he said.

He was in London promoting a book called *Alan Shearer's Diary of a Season*. It isn't going to win a

Pulitzer prize, but offers intriguing insights into the life of a professional footballer, particularly when it demonstrates the manner in which the modern soccer star is both revered and abused.

Shearer is particularly unpopular with Manchester United fans, who call him a 'greedy bastard' because they believe he turned down going to Old Trafford after an offer of better wages from Blackburn. It happens not to be true, but it doesn't make any difference.

'The fact is I never talked to Manchester United. The only club to offer a deal was Blackburn, and that is where I went. It makes me smile when I read Manchester United fans worrying about the hostile reception Eric Cantona gets. What about the abuse I get at Manchester?' he said.

I asked him if he ever felt like going into the crowd like Eric did. 'Sometimes, when you go to retrieve a ball, you can spot them in the crowd, make eye contact. I just walk away. Not worth it, is it?' he said. He should have a word with Eric.

His worst moment came in Dublin, when the international against Ireland was abandoned because of

crowd behaviour. Shearer was standing in the corridor outside the England dressing room, watching the casualties of the crowd violence being brought in.

'There was a little boy, no more than eight years of age, brought in with his mother. I thought I'd try to help, so I went to him and said, "I'm Alan Shearer, how are you, son?" and he said, "I effing hate you."' I asked what he did. 'I said "sorry" and walked away.'

He ruminates on the curious mixture of hero-worship and hatred that goes with being a football star.

'We are paid a lot of money nowadays and are treated like pop stars, so we have to know how to behave. The big difference is, of course, the pop stars, and the rest, aren't supposed to be part of the community and mix with the crowd. We are, and sometimes that's where the trouble starts.

'With that little boy, all I was trying to do was to be nice, to use my fame to cheer him up. The worst thing was his mother just stood there while he abused me. Didn't say a thing. Perhaps that's what's wrong nowadays. No child of mine would behave like that. If it did, and I saw it, it wouldn't happen again,' he said.

Gordon Taylor, chief executive of the Professional Footballers Association, thinks Shearer, like Gary Lineker before him, is the perfect example for youngsters.

'He's become a flagship for football, not just for his performances, but by his behaviour off the field. If all players behaved like Shearer, my job would be a lot easier,' he said.

It was good to meet him and not be disappointed. He is an impressive young man. It is difficult to believe he is only twenty-four and some way from his footballing prime. The real lesson other players and their masters could learn from Shearer is that he lights the way to a better future, only because he treads softly in the footpath of those who did the job before him.

August 1995

Alan Shearer retired from international football in 2000 after captaining England in their unsuccessful European Championship finals campaign. He continued to play for Newcastle, where he moved from Blackburn in 1996.

IN PRAISE OF THE
PENALTY SHOOT-OUT

I CANNOT understand the condemnation of the penalty shoot-out. In a season short of real quality and excitement, the sight of professional footballers having a nervous breakdown at the thought of shooting a ball past a stationary opponent from only twelve yards away has offered thrills and not a little amusement.

There is, for instance, much humour in a situation where a man who is paid a few grand a week to kick a football – a man bulging with vitamins and health, rubbed down with oils, honed and greased to perfection – is required to undertake the simple task of a penalty kick and succeeds only in hitting the corner flag. It is soccer's equivalent of the banana-skin joke and, as such, has a place in a game that has increasingly revealed its links with the best days of music hall.

What is more, it is my considered opinion that two teams who have played against each other for four hours without settling matters have been pratting about and could not complain if the match was decided on who had the ugliest manager.

What the shoot-out gives the fan is something like the excitement and tension of the final putt in the Ryder Cup or a Wimbledon tie-breaker. There is one difference – scoring a penalty has to be easier. It is the equivalent of sinking a six-foot putt into a hole as big as a dustbin, or of playing a tie-break against an opponent with one leg. Should any soccer player think otherwise and find it difficult to hit a target that is somewhat larger than the average barn door, then he hasn't got time to play in a Cup final. He should be at home practising penalty kicks.

There would be little need for penalty shoot-outs if the players knew where the goal was. Apart from the splendid Gary Lineker (now there's a chap who knows about public relations) I've seen few players who frighten goalkeepers and cause havoc in the penalty box.

The trouble is that too many people get involved in the box nowadays. We've got overlapping full-backs and players 'arriving from midfield' all crowding into an area that is already bursting with wingers tackling back, inside-forwards playing like full-backs and centre-forwards marking centre-halves.

Modern goalmouths resemble the departure lounge at Gatwick on a bank holiday. It is time we returned to those dear departed days when the penalty box was owned by the centre-half and the only opponent allowed within its confines was the opposing centre-forward. That was when we had gladiators, put on earth to knock the bejasus out of one another. If you saw Syd Bycroft take on Wally Ardron you would know what I mean.

Bycroft was Doncaster's centre-half, a man of saturnine good looks, centre parting, brilliantined head and dangerous dark eyes. Ardron was Rotherham's centre-forward, wavy haired, broad browed, his body carved from the coal face. He was made from anthracite.

When these two met, the Doncaster penalty box was no place for the faint-hearted. I imagine that when the Good Lord made them he took them on one side and said, 'Now Wally and Syd, I have made you to go forth and kick lumps off each other to entertain the good folk of South Yorkshire.' And they did as they were told. In any list of hard men, they would be in the top ten, and it would be a brave man who required confirmation of their claims.

I met Syd Bycroft a while ago and we talked of those days. He reckoned Wally was one of the hardest he had to deal with, but there were a few around in his time who constituted a handful.

He told me that he had been greatly helped in his job of seeing off opposing centre-forwards by the introduction of lights at Doncaster. The club had them some time before they became commonplace and because they had yet to be perfected, there were parts of the Doncaster ground the lights failed to illuminate.

'There was one bit down by the corner flag which was pitch black,' said Bycroft. 'I used to lure them down there and do a bit of damage I can tell you. It was lovely.'

That was a long time before penalty shoot-outs, when football players had their own way of settling matters.

April 1992

SMITH'S PRINCIPLES
WEARING WELL IN CHANGING
FOOTBALL FASHION

THE FIRST football joke I ever heard was about a manager. Angus Seed, in charge at Barnsley in the days when Danny Blanchflower cost £6,000 and people living near Oakwell charged two pence to park your bike, was seen walking to work one day carrying a record player. He was stopped by a fan who looked quizzically at his burden. 'I got it for the players,' explained Seed. 'Tha's been robbed,' said the fan. That relationship with the fans, the gallows humour, is about the only factor linking Angus Seed and the managers of his day with their modern counterparts.

When Seed ruled Barnsley, footballers knew their place. Tommy Lawton told a story about asking to see Theo Kelly, the secretary-manager of Everton, to request a transfer. At the appointed time Tommy knocked on his door and opened it. As he stepped inside the office, Kelly yelled, 'Stop.' He instructed Lawton to go back outside the room, to knock again and not to enter until told to do so. He was then told that having entered the room he must stand on a mat near the door until summoned to approach Kelly's desk.

Lawton, an England international at the time, did as he was told. When he finally arrived in front of the manager he told him he wanted a transfer, whereupon Kelly said, 'You want a transfer? I've been trying to give you away for four months. Now go away through the door, close it quietly behind you, go about your training and don't waste my time.' Tommy said he felt belittled but at the same time grateful he escaped with his life.

The transmutation of managers in the time spanned by the careers of Lawton and Alan Shearer is as much a social history of Britain as the story of a developing game. The mores of our society from the forties to the nineties are seen most clearly in the story of football management, from Stan Cullis, through Busby, Shankly and Ramsey to Clough, Allison and Revie, on to Ferguson, Dalglish and Keegan, and not forgetting the significant contribution of George Graham.

Any comparison between Angus Seed and Kenny Dalglish would have to conclude they were alike only because they both stood upright and wore clothes. Today's manager is as important to the corporate image of the club as the star striker. He no longer leads what used to be called 'the backroom team'. Now he is the

star name on the letterhead of the prospectus that will transform his club into a public company.

When Newcastle went in search of a replacement for Kevin Keegan, they were looking for a figure to please both the City and the terraces. Managers such as Joe Kinnear, who has worked wonders with Wimbledon and ought to be one of the most sought after, was never mentioned. Another manager who didn't stay by the phone when he heard Newcastle wanted to replace Keegan was Jim Smith.

He has been a manager for twenty-five years. It has been a continuous occupation except for a three-month spell as chief executive of the Football League Managers' Association. He left that job in 1995 to take Derby County into the Premier League. Jim Smith has managed nine clubs – Boston United, Colchester United, Blackburn Rovers, Birmingham City, Oxford United, Queens Park Rangers, Newcastle United, Portsmouth and now Derby County. In all that time he has been what one observer called 'a beacon of humanity in an increasingly joyless business'. He has also improved matters at every club he has managed. He took Oxford from Third to First Division, guided Queens Park Rangers to a League Cup final and fifth position in the old First Division. But perhaps his major achievement has been to be universally admired and liked in a notoriously bitchy occupation.

He has had his moments, particularly at Newcastle. When he arrived he was greeted with a headline which said that when Sir John Hall took over at Newcastle his first job would be to sack Jim Smith – which was why he didn't hold his breath when Keegan left. He realises he doesn't fit the profile required by the money men to attract investors to a glamorous club like Newcastle.

Ron Atkinson christened Jim Smith 'Old Bald Eagle' but he was wrong. Anthropomorphically speaking he's more of a shire horse than a bird of prey. He is built for grafting, not for soaring. He was born in Shiregreen in Yorkshire and always wanted to be a footballer. He joined his father as a wheelwright. Dad said, 'You'd better get them feet going because your hands are useless.' He says his father's observation motivates him even today.

He played for Sheffield United when Joe Mercer was manager. 'He wore a different suit every day. I thought, "One day I'll have some of that." He also coached with a smile on his face and I've never forgotten that either,' he said. Smith played for Sheffield United, Aldershot, Halifax Town and Lincoln City. Graham Taylor, who was also at Lincoln, remembered him as 'a ball-playing right-half who cared for the game and had great enthusiasm and honesty'. It is alleged that when Ron Gray, manager of Lincoln, approached Alan Ball senior, manager of Halifax, for Jim Smith, the two managers played snooker for the fee. It cost Mr Gray £500.

Jim Smith started his management career with Boston. He did everything, including running the lottery, acting as secretary, digging drains, concreting the car park and decorating the boardroom. He says he must have done a good job because when he went back to Boston eight years after leaving, they still had the same wallpaper. As well as Mercer he has found inspiration in the way Ron Greenwood, Bobby Robson and Bill Shankly approached the job of manager. He admired their enthusiasm, their lack of cynicism and, above all, the way their teams played.

Jim Smith's teams have always played intelligent, skilful football. He says he only once tried to kick his way out of trouble and that was when he was manager of Blackburn and played against Luton with one man up front and the rest in a do-or-die defence. The team achieved a much-needed draw but Smith was so ashamed at what he saw that he apologised to the Luton manager and vowed never to play that way again. Nor has he.

When he reflects on his life in football management, he sees more clearly than most how the job has changed.

'I'm from the generation of managers who did it all – transfers, coaching, administration, driving the team bus if necessary. The new manager is more of a coach. That's no bad thing. The secret of the job is being adaptable. It's like the relationship managers have with players. I doubt if young players today feel about their manager the way I felt about Joe Mercer.

'Managers nowadays don't have the same respect or control they once had. They don't have the power because apart from the difference in the way young people are brought up, there is the question of money. The salaries being paid now alter things. Bound to.'

Similarly, he sees the emergence of the new, glamorous and financially independent managers such as Keegan, Dalglish, Souness, Robson and Hoddle as being another significant shift.

Jim Smith has survived a quarter of a century in a risky and fickle occupation by changing when he had to without sacrificing his basic principles. As much as he loves his job, he sees it as a lonely, isolating occupation.

'You are at the beck and call of everyone yet on your own. You move about so much there is little time for solid friendships. Pubs are out because there is always someone there who will collar you about football and what you are doing wrong. So why do I bother? In bad times I ask myself that and always have the same answer. I am still in football because I love it as much now as I did when I first came into the game.'

A lot has happened to football in the twenty-five years Smith has been a manager. When he started, Brian Clough was manager at Derby County, Bobby Moore made his 100th international appearance for England and Liverpool, under Shankly, won the First Division championship. Shankly is long gone, so are Matt and Jock Stein, and a sighting of Brian Clough is treated as a rare event.

In the last quarter of a century, football has changed more rapidly and radically than at any other time in its long history. In all the glitz and glamour of the modern game it is easy to perceive someone like Jim Smith as an outdated, old-fashioned figure. Yet the fact is the new executives have much to learn from this penny-plain man. His honest, down-to-earth and, above all, affable approach to his job sets an example to those who follow. Amid all the ballyhoo and confusion, it is important to have men around who know the difference between love and money, sport and showbiz, men like Jim Smith who are football fans rather than speculators on the stock market.

January 1997

Jim Smith steered Derby County to Premiership survival in their penultimate fixture of 2000–01 with an away victory over the champions, Manchester United. Then aged sixty, Smith still had a year left on his contract, after which he was 'virtually certain' to retire.

PLATT'S ASCENSION TO NATIONAL HERO A SALUTARY TALE OF HONEST ENDEAVOUR

THERE WAS A MINUTE of extra time left when Gazza took a free kick on the right-hand side of the Belgian penalty area. It was crowded in the box. David Platt moved from his marker to find a yard of space. The defender stayed where he was. The ball dropped over Platt's shoulder and as it did he swivelled and hit what they used to describe as 'a fulminating shot past the hapless custodian'. It took England to the quarter-final of Italia '90 and to a luckless semi-final against Germany. It did more for David Platt – it changed his life forever. It transformed an anonymous member of the England squad into a national hero. It made the substitute a star and transported him from an icy flat in Crewe, where he could keep warm only by wearing his training gear in bed, to a castle overlooking the Mediterranean, one the home of Lord Byron. In between times, the lad from Chadderton, Lancashire, became the world's most expensive footballer. Clubs in England and Italy have paid more than £22 million for his talent. You could say he has done well.

He is twenty-nine years old, exceedingly rich, and fit as a butcher's dog. When I say he is in good condition,

I don't mean in that aerobic, bulging-thighed, lunchbox-proud kind of way, but the real thing, where the body fairly hums with energy. You feel that if you put a bulb in his mouth it would light up. He carries the obligatory mobile phone and wears a wristwatch costing as much as a small car.

He is both friendly and articulate, but in a slightly guarded fashion. He has written a book about his life so far. His autobiography is a rarity in football in that he wrote it himself and there is nothing in its pages to make the tabloids reach for their chequebooks. It is a straightforward account of an extraordinary career. Ask him to sum it up and he says he has got where he is by 'hard work, luck, a little talent and *the* goal'. Scoring against Belgium was the defining moment of his life. He is shown on the cover of the book the moment after he scored, his face gleaming with joy, his arms outstretched in celebration. Even now he finds it difficult to explain how he felt. The picture tells it all, he says. Photographers have asked him to reproduce the smile. He can't do it. In any case, he is a professional footballer, not a male model. He doesn't say that, but you feel he would if he wasn't so polite.

The most revealing sentence in the book is: 'In my opinion, it is more important to be judged as a person than a player.' He says he came to this conclusion upon the death of Bobby Moore, when he saw how a nation responded to a man who was as modest on the street as he was commanding on the field of play. It is a sure sign of changing mores in our society that once upon a time – and not too long ago – anyone expressing the opinion that heroes on the pitch might also be decent members of society would be accused of stating the obvious. Today, it would greatly help the ugly image of football if Platt's observation was framed and hung in every player's locker, not to mention every manager's office.

Platt says, 'It is easy for people to admire you for what you do on a pitch, much more difficult for people to admire you for what you are . . . It is important for footballers nowadays to understand what and who they are. They are not just athletes but entertainers and celebrities. They are treated like showbiz personalities. Soccer is on the front page. Players don't just appear on 'Match of the Day'. It is difficult for some players to be thrust into the spotlight.

'Young apprentices, sixteen to eighteen, are sent off to college once a week to learn how to manage a leisure centre if things go wrong. Perhaps they should be taught about media relations and the rest. I don't think anyone has yet addressed the problem. I was lucky, I had a step-by-step career – YTS with Manchester United,

Third Division with Crewe, Second Division with Aston Villa, then Italy.

'When I was at Manchester United, I saw people like Bryan Robson and Ray Wilkins and chose them as my role models. They didn't let me down. They influenced me in a positive way. I saw how they conducted themselves. But I could easily have chosen someone else who might have influenced me in a different way. No one told me. I made my own choice. There is no one at a club who answers the question, "How did they get there?" Maybe if there was, that would help. What I feel about myself now is if I do it right both on and off the field, and have success, then others looking at me might get it right.'

He says that the only time he felt his 'fame slipping out of control' was in the aftermath of Italia '90, when brief chats with local journalists turned into three-hour press conferences with the international media and he felt for the first time the incessant heat of the spotlight.

'In a moment, I had gone from being a player at a Birmingham club to being world-renowned. I hadn't grown up into what I was. I had to catch up with my image,' he said. He sought the help of a psychologist. 'Did me the world of good. I went to him for twelve months and told him all my fears and worries. I was particularly concerned about my change of status and the way it affected those close to me. For instance, before I scored that goal, I would join a team discussion and make a point without it seeming big-headed, whereas I felt that, if I made the same suggestion with my new-found celebrity, people would think, "Who does he think he is? Big head!" It was not so much the way fame might change me, but the way it would affect the attitude of other people towards me.'

Did it work, I wondered. It obviously had, but I just thought I'd ask. He thought for a moment, then replied, 'It taught me to take control of my own mind.'

Italy completed his education. He lapped it up. Not for him food parcels from home or a nostalgic refuge in the nearest bar selling Tetleys. He loved the food, learned the language and embraced the lifestyle. He was fascinated by the Italian passion for the game; at first intrigued and then convinced by the way Italian foot-ballers trained and conducted their lives.

I said that what comes across in the book is that his Italian team-mates seemed much more mature and sophisticated than their British counterparts. He said he didn't believe that to be true. However, it is difficult to imagine a scenario in any club in Britain such as he describes at Bari where, after training, he and members of the team would sit in a restaurant and talk about events in Bosnia and the rest of the world. He says it is the difference between a restaurant culture and one based round the pub; the difference between a meal and a piss-up, though he didn't say that either.

What he did say was that the main difference between Italian and British football was that the Italians were tactically and technically superior because they didn't have to play as many games. They were also within a system that encouraged players to work on their techniques and prepare both mentally and physically.

'Take Alan Shearer,' he said. 'With European and midweek matches, he hasn't had a rest so far this season – no opportunity to practise and work on technique.

'In Italy, we played on Sunday, went in on Monday when the game was still fresh in our minds and had Tuesday off. But then it was double training on Wednesday. Thursday afternoon we trained then started the build-up to Sunday, gearing up mentally for the game. Our system doesn't allow that. Mental tiredness creeps in.'

I said that was all very well, but it seemed to me that some of our players lacked even the basic requirement of being able to kick with either foot. He had made himself a two-footed player, why hadn't one or two of his team-mates? He conceded that there might be a case for spending an extra fifteen minutes or so in training, learning a further use for a limb other than standing on it. He said that in Italy the players would automatically take extra time to improve their skills.

'They are more professional. I'm not saying our players are unprofessional. It's simply that in Italy, footballers seem able to say to themselves, "This is my job and I'll work at it so I become a better player."'

Any player who under-achieves and settles for second best could learn a lot from David Platt. I have a feeling he might make a formidable manager.

'I want to manage Sampdoria. That is my dream,' he says. 'I haven't had my fill of Italy by a long way. Playing at Sampdoria was the best two years of my life, and not just in soccer terms. So I'd like to go back there and then finish up back home in England.' He doesn't say this in a dreamy, wistful fashion but in a positive, determined way. What he has learned in his journey through life is that you can wish on dreams all you like, but only if you work hard at them do they come true.

November 1995

David Platt fulfilled his ambition to coach Sampdoria in 1998–99 but lasted just six games (none of which was won) before being replaced as the club struggled unsuccessfully to avoid relegation from *Serie A*. He later managed Nottingham Forest, leaving in 2001 to take charge of England's Under-21 team.

Up a gum tree

'God rest ye merry gentlemen, let nothing you dismay; no scandal, bung or violence upsets the old FA' could perhaps open the Lancaster Gate Christmas concert. A second tune might start: 'From the first day of the season the true fan has to see ... Three wide men, two nosey hacks and a game stuck up a gum tree.'

Scene: Lancaster Gate, the home of football, the setting for a Christmas concert that attracted the biggest gathering of football identities since the Old Bailey. The media were not invited but a *Daily Telegraph* reporter disguised as a wine waiter gained access and this is his report:

The entertainment began with Sir Bert Millichip, Graham Kelly and David Davies, sometimes known as the Three Wise Men of the FA, appearing on stage riding donkeys. They were accompanied by Eric Hall, the agent, riding an ass. All together to the tune of 'We Three Kings of Orient Are':

> We three Kings of Lancaster Gate,
> Have an awful lot on our plate.
> Bungs and butting,
> Players rutting,
> When will it all abate?
>
> Oh, oh, Harry Harris, Mihir Bose,
> Whatever next do you suppose?

> Allegations, accusations,
> Where it all ends heaven knows.

DAVID DAVIES (solo):
> Venables has no chance to shine,
> The press conspire to seek his decline,
> They are cruel,
> He's a jewel,
> And an old mate of mine.

ALL TOGETHER:
> Oh, oh, Harry Harris, Mihir Bose etc.

SIR BERT MILLICHIP (solo):
> My name is Bert and I'm very astute,
> I let them think I'm irresolute,
> Diving and ducking,
> Meaningless clucking,
> Like my hero King Canute.

ALL TOGETHER:
> Oh, oh, Harry Harris, Mihir Bose, etc.

GRAHAM KELLY (solo):
> People say that soccer's mendacious,
> Management weak and the players rapacious,
> What can I do when the whole crew,
> Is bibulous and disgracious?

ALL TOGETHER:
> Oh, oh, Harry Harris, Mihir Bose,
> Whatever next will they expose?
> Why can't they be like our committee,
> Incompetent and comatose?

The trio left the stage to tumultuous applause. Joe Royle and Peter Johnson, the Everton chairman, moved among the crowd collecting money for footballers who have been the victims of the legal system. A pipe band played while the collection took place.

There was a standing ovation for the next performance which featured Duncan Ferguson, Paul Gascoigne and Eric Cantona singing their tribute to George Graham, another who had contributed greatly to the image of British football throughout the year.

FERGUSON, GASCOIGNE AND CANTONA (dressed as angels to the tune of 'Good King Wenceslas'):

> Good King Venables looked out,
> On the feast of Stephen,
> Loads of money strewn about,
> Deep and crisp and even.
> 'What a lovely sight,' he said,
> With a smile so jolly,
> When George Graham came in sight,
> Scooping up the lolly.
>
> ''Ere,' said Tel, 'you can't do that,
> You don't know where it came from,
> You'll need a bill including VAT
> Or Bill will put the arm on.
> Come inside and have a drink,
> We will have a party,
> There's someone you ought to meet,
> Name of Eddie Ashby.'

But George was busy with his sack
Scooping up the honey.
He was too involved to see
The money might be funny.
When the day of reckoning came
Georgie made a statement.
He said, 'It's a funny game,'
And blamed it on his agent.

Then, to the general amusement of those foregathered,
the three troubadours gave their solo versions of coup-
lets learned in childhood which they used when carol
singing.

DUNCAN FERGUSON:

Hole in my stocking, hole in my clog,
Give us a penny or I'll heid your dog.

PAUL GASCOIGNE:

Hole in my stocking, hole in my clothes,
Give us a penny or I'll nutt your nose.

ERIC CANTONA:

Hole in my stocking, hole in my shoe,
Donnez-moi a franc or I'll kung-fu vous.

At this point, the Minister for Transport presented the
Hackney Cab Award for Passenger of the Year to Dennis
Wise, of Chelsea and England. The members of the
Premier League commission into bungs received a
special award from a grateful game for the longest-ever
inquiry into a four-letter word.

The climax of the evening was a massed choir of Premier League chairmen and football supporters led by Rick Parry (chief executive of the Premier League) and the Sky Television Concert Orchestra conducted by Rupert Murdoch.

CHAIRMEN (to the tune of 'While Shepherds Watched Their Flocks by Night'):

> While chairmen watched their teams each week,
> Assessing what they'd got,
> An angel from TV came down
> And nicked the bloody lot.
> It used to be the people's game,
> A servant of their wish.
> But nowadays it's disappeared,
> Unless you own a dish.
>
> Fear not said Rupert Murdoch's man,
> We'll fill your vaults with lolly,
> And you can help a needy cause,
> Like a rise for poor Stan Colly.
>
> The Premier League's a lovely place,
> With money it's awash,
> The rest of them can bugger off
> And leave you with the dosh.
> A good idea the chairmen said,
> Unanimously so,
> The other teams in lower leagues
> Can pack their bags and go.

SUPPORTERS:
> The men who run our national game,
> Are fools and uninspired.
> The best news for us football fans,
> Is that they've all been fired.
> But wait a mo' it's Christmas time,
> Perhaps we didn't oughta.
> Except they'll always get a job,
> Employed by Yorkshire Water.

At the end of the evening, Sir Bert Millichip announced that Terry Venables had been appointed England coach until the year 2050. He also mentioned that the new technical director of coaching to succeed Charles Hughes would be Cilla Black.

Graham Kelly brought proceedings to a fitting end by announcing that England had been awarded first place in a new European competition to find the country whose players do most spitting during the course of a match. Kelly said this would do much to compensate for an otherwise disappointing year in Europe.

He said that in his letter of commendation, the FIFA Commissioner for Expectoration had said there was only one country in it. He said the judges were particularly impressed by the English players' ability to spit and talk at the same time and said their skill at spitting while talking was literally breathtaking.

Mr Kelly said this proved that practice makes perfect. He said he had noticed an improvement in the ability of English players to snot from either nostril. While it may be true that most of our players couldn't kick with both feet, when it came to snotting we had more two-nostril players than anyone in the world.

It was in a state of celebration and jubilation not witnessed since 1966 that the gathering repaired to Terry Venables's club for an evening of karaoke, a head-butting competition and other harmless fun. The club is to be purchased by Mrs Bottomley for a grateful nation.

December 1995

WHY DO REFS STAY IN THE JOB DESPITE ALL THE FOUL INSULTS?

WHY WOULD ANYONE want to become a football referee? It remains one of life's great unsolved mysteries, like why people eat tripe and the function of the human appendix. Even the most respected referees have the popularity rating of a man towing a caravan down a narrow road on a bank holiday weekend.

They certainly don't do it for the money. Today Philip Don will be at Maine Road, Manchester. The £300 he is paid will hardly make a dent in the gate receipts or enable him to contemplate a change of lifestyle. It is, however, considerably more than he receives for refereeing in Europe – £300 more, to be precise. All he gets for being in charge of important games on the Continent is £75 per day living allowance.

He has been refereeing since he was fourteen. He is now forty-two years old. In his time, he has been punched by a player in the Chiswick Sunday League, smuggled out of Fratton Park in the back of a van, and earned his own place in the Dictionary of Cheap Jibes (Referee's Edition) when Jimmy Greaves, commenting on the sending off of Tony Adams for a professional foul, said the Arsenal captain had been well and truly 'P Don' (geddit?).

If you didn't, the pupils at the South London school where Don is headmaster most certainly did. The children are in favour of having a boss who is a famous referee. It gives them something to talk about. 'That was never a sending-off offence,' they say on Monday morning. At parents' days and school functions, parents are more eager to talk football than discuss the academic progress of their children.

Philip Don lives with his wife, Judith, also a teacher, in a quiet cul-de-sac in Surrey. Judith doesn't enjoy going to football matches. 'I get upset at the names they call Philip,' she says. They have a daughter at Oxford and a son who is a member of the British triathlon team.

Philip Don is a slender, wiry man. He runs twenty miles a week to keep in shape. Even on holiday he trained for fifteen of the twenty-one days they were away. He is attractive, has an affable manner, and is not the sort of person you would expect to be publicly reviled as a 'w****r' or a b*****d', which he is most Saturdays as a matter of routine. Nor is he the kind of bloke you would imagine being escorted from the ground by a platoon of policemen to save him being scragged by the mob. The question is, why bother?

'I don't really have a good answer,' he says. 'It started when I was fourteen. I'd play soccer in the morning and then referee a game in the afternoon. When I was at college, I'd supplement my grant by refereeing three games a week. So was it the case I became a referee because I'm a mercenary Yorkshireman? Don't think so. Not even our worst enemies could accuse us of doing it for the money.' He placed his fingertips together. He has neat hands. 'I've always been a methodical and organised person. I've always captained teams I've played in. Maybe refereeing is an extension of that. Power. Maybe that's it. Maybe I get a kick out of being in control.'

He was born in Hull. There is a trace of an accent. His ambition to be a referee was sorely tested before his first game when he had to clean mountains of cowpats from the pitch before play could commence. As he moved up the divisions, he observed the crowds became bigger and the surroundings more spectacular but the referee's status rarely improved on someone who was expected to shovel manure. At one league ground, Don had to ask for an air freshener because the room set aside for the referee was the annexe to a public urinal. At another, the officials changed in the laundry room and in another the pre-match briefing by the referee could be carried out only if a linesman stood in the shower. The ultimate insult was invented by the club that built a palatial new stand and forgot to include a room for the officials in the plans.

Working in Europe, he discovered that visiting referees were treated with splendid generosity, which lasted only so long as the home team won. In Oporto, he allowed a goal that the home team believed was offside. Oporto lost 2–1. That night at the official banquet, Philip Don and his linesmen were placed between two television sets that showed continuous replays of the controversial goal all night long.

He thinks, however, that the status of the referee is changing for the better and the World Cup in the United States is responsible.

'It showed the crucial part referees have to play in the way the game is played,' he said. 'The laws weren't changed. All that FIFA did was to remind referees of what their responsibilities are.

'Something had to be done to make the game more entertaining. In this country, people were paying a lot of money and not much of what they saw was worth the price of admission. There seemed to be too much pressure on management and players to be negative and forget about the spectators. I believe FIFA and the referees changed all that.

'Most importantly, FIFA have allowed referees to appear on the media to explain their problems and what they're trying to do. I'm all in favour of it. At one time, all that referees were allowed to say was "no comment". Now we have a much more important profile and it can only lead to greater understanding between all of us responsible for making sure the game gives value for money.

'It will take a season or two for the game to come to terms with the new philosophy, and what we referees have to do in the meantime is achieve consistency. We have to convince managers and players that this is what we're after. If we do, we'll have their full co-operation. As referees, we have to hold regular meetings, watch videos, work out a consistent approach. Most import-antly, if we are wrong and the video evidence tells us we are, we should own up.

'This question of consistency is where the argument for two referees falls down. It's difficult enough with one but what sort of consistency would be achieved with two refs at the same game? It would be mayhem. My own view is that the system of three officials has stood the test of time.'

Hasn't the time come when being a referee should be considered a full-time job? Last season Philip Don had nine weeks' unpaid leave from his school. He was not recompensed for loss of earnings. He thinks there might be a case for paying referees more money but not for them becoming full-time officials.

'I'm sure that if I announced I had become a full-time referee, spectators and players alike would expect me to become a better referee overnight,' he said. 'The truth might be that if I had a five-year contract with good money, pension, life assurance and all that, I might become complacent. As it is, on my present one-year contract, I'm always striving for perfection. I have to because I know that if I slip, next year I'm officiating on Hackney Marshes.'

He thinks the greatest virtue of the present system is that it brings to the game people who possess skills and insights gained in a broad area of man-management. Nor does he believe, in the final analysis, that the job deserves full-time, professional status.

'I suppose I was living like a full-time referee in

America during the World Cup, in that I had nothing else to do,' he said. 'And that was the problem. After I had trained, looked at videos of my last game, prepared for the next, there was nothing left to do. It was boring.'

Nonetheless, it is a fact that the present system depends on the co-operation of employers and a satisfactory balance being maintained between a job and a hobby. It is this that has led to something of a crisis in Philip Don's life.

'My problem is that the hobby is taking over the job. I had nine weeks' unpaid leave last year and it's getting to the stage where the governors and staff might be saying that I'm not spending enough time at school. I'll have to sit down and think about what to do. I have already turned down one trip to Europe this year because it comes in school time. If I turn down too many games, I'll be taken off the list. So what do I do, resign?'

He leaves the question unanswered. In the coming months, he has some serious thinking to do. But at the end of the day, the reason why he decided to become a referee is much more fascinating and difficult to explain than why he is thinking about chucking in the job. So let's try again. Why on earth did you want to be a referee?

'When I was in charge of the Cup final, my mother reminded me that when I was a teenager I told her that one day I'd referee a final at Wembley,' he said. 'I'd forgotten that. Obviously, the ambition has always been with me but I've never tried to explain it. Again I ask myself, is it power? Or might it be something else? I became a teacher because I had a sense of vocation. For a while, when I was young, I thought I might have a vocation for the priesthood. So maybe being a referee is vocational, too.'

He was smiling when he said it but it might be right. It could be that the most perplexing of questions has a simple answer. It is not that a man chooses to be a referee; the fact is, he can't help it.

August 1994

Philip Don refereed a Premiership fixture for the final time in 1995. After giving up his job as a head teacher, he became Referees Officer to the FA Premier League. In 2001 he headed the Professional Game Match Officials Board, which oversaw the introduction of twenty-four full-time referees.

SECOND DIVISION OF
WORLD FOOTBALL

YOU CAN ALWAYS TELL when things are getting really desperate by the way people start banging on about wearing the England shirt with pride and getting the players to bellow the national anthem. Dr Johnson (who should be alive at such a time and planning to take over the job of chief executive at the Football Association) was only partly right when he observed that patriotism was the last refuge of a scoundrel. It is also the last resort of a lost cause.

When we hear a sensible and intelligent man like Kevin Keegan talking about the three lions and Paul Gascoigne in the same breath, you understand why he wants a job with an ejector seat. Why does he want the job at all? He was quoted as saying England against France were 'crap'. He was right. Nothing has changed since. So why bother?

He knows that huffing and puffing will get you so far but gone are the days when all we had to do was stick out our chests and work on the principle that our opponents didn't like the glint of cold steel. Our faults have little to do with character; they are more about lack of technique and skill.

I watched Mr Keegan's press conference on television but didn't hear anyone ask him why we were outclassed by the French and if he thought our present squad were

Kevin Keegan

capable of winning a cup at either European or world level, and if not then why not.

As we have said a thousand times before, the speculation and pontification surrounding the choice of England coach matters not a toot. It is a media ritual, a dance of ever-decreasing circles. It will remain so until we create a system of producing players capable of beating the rest of the world at football rather than a competition for who can sing the national anthem loudest.

That said, I am looking forward to Mr Keegan's stint. We should manage the likes of Bulgaria, Poland and Sweden. By that I mean they are teams like us, from the second division of world football, and if we can't get a result from them there will be a strong case for Dale Winton becoming England boss with Danny La Rue as his goalkeeping coach.

Supposing Mr Keegan's team win all four games with him in charge. Might he change his mind? He says maybe but it is difficult to believe such a self-confessed patriot would abandon his country at a critical moment in our history.

I have a question on behalf of the nation, but I want it set to music. I want the massed bands of the Brigade of Guards at Wembley, the Huddersfield Choral Society singing 'Jerusalem' and 70,000 fans waving Union flags while I ask Mr Keegan: Queen and country, or Fayed and Fulham? A knight or a knave? Or, to put it bluntly in tabloid speak, would he rather be remembered as a turnip or a traitor?

*　　*　　*

Chelsea are to re-lay their pitch because it has become 'sticky underfoot'. So too, and for the same reasons, are Manchester United. No wonder. Whenever you see a close-up of a player on television, he is spitting. This happens at least once a minute so no wonder the pitches are soggy.

A correspondent, Mr Morgan, says he has discovered why today's players are paid so much more. 'Would you, even for £20,000 per week, go out in front of thousands of people, say twice a week, and continually dive into a bath of someone's spittle and phlegm?' He argues that once players are made aware of what they are doing, it might have an effect on the number of them deliberately falling over in the penalty area.

I thank Mr Morgan for an important and thoughtful contribution to the ongoing debate about football. I treasure his conclusion: 'Maybe a health inspector will rule the game "unhygienic".' Football unfit for human consumption. Cool, or what?

February 1999

Do politicians really care about football?

THE DUBLINER BAR in Phoenix is at the junction of 41st and Thunderbird. I just mention that in case you are ever in Arizona and feel the need to drink a decent pint of Guinness while watching English football on television. I saw the Wembley game against Scotland. At least the weather was good and the booze helped numb the pain.

I stood alongside a man dressed in a kilt and a Rod Stewart wig, which was a distinct improvement on the last time I stood next to a Scottish supporter. It was that notorious game at Wembley when they nicked our goalposts and my companion was wearing a tam o'shanter, Wellington boots and a cardboard box held over his private parts by tartan suspenders.

Since that day, games against the Auld Enemy have been rationed to special occasions. On the evidence of what we saw at Wembley, this has served to protect the myth that England are the superior soccer nation. We used to say if you think England are bad wait until you see Scotland. The sad boast no longer holds up. What's depressing is to return home and find that people are seeking scapegoats instead of facing the truth. It is no good blaming Shearer or suggesting that because of his supposed tactical naivety Mr Keegan needs help.

Shearer is far from his best but the service he gets is lousy and who is better? Emile Heskey? I think not. Andy Cole or Robbie Fowler? Not convincing at international level. But as with Shearer, the problem remains: who is going to give them the ball? Similarly, who are these masterminds to help Kevin Keegan transform his selling platers into Derby winners? Terry Venables? Ho, hum. Glenn Hoddle? Ho, double hum. If they were miracle workers we wouldn't be in our present situation, which is freefall without a parachute. Mr Keegan and the rest of us will be old bones before we produce a football team capable of winning the World Cup.

The present bunch lack intelligence as well as skill. They are under-achievers because they are under-developed both as human beings and professional athletes. They provide the most obvious spectacular evidence of our being a second-rate sporting nation. It is as if the rest of the world passed them by some time ago. Why? Look no further than the system – or rather the lack of one – producing our athletes. This is one of my pet subjects but I will return to it again and again because nothing will change until we make the poli-

ticians see how short-sighted and gormless they have been and continue to be.

For all Mr Blair's honeyed words, we still sell off playing fields. We send our children to schools 94 per cent of which don't have a gymnasium – third-world England. A recent survey revealed that 40 per cent of girls and 20 per cent of boys drop out of school sports by the age of fourteen because it spoils their hair, makes them sweaty and is 'uncool'. Have you ever heard anything so daft and depressing?

The real reason children back away when they are given the opportunity to do so is because the system is at best half-hearted and at worst downright apathetic to the concept of sport as an important factor in their education.

The Government says things will get better when they put 600 new 'sports co-ordinators' in place. That's like sending snow ploughs to Arizona, or England cricketers to South Africa. Wouldn't it be better if we built playing fields instead of selling them, put physical education on the school curriculum instead of shilly shallying, acted instead of postured?

Returning from Phoenix, it wasn't just the weather I found depressing. The story of the new Wembley Stadium seems the perfect paradigm of the shambles that is English sport. Instead of schmoozing the Football Association, giving millions of Lottery money to Wembley National Stadium plc, doting on parasites from FIFA and the Olympic movement and spending more millions on silly bids for overblown sporting events, why doesn't Chris Smith (the Minister for Sport) put serious money where it will do most good, which is to say at the grass roots of sport?

Like all politicians, Mr Blair and his lot are good at banging on about the future. In sporting terms, it will only be improved if our children are given more encouragement and support. I don't care about Olympic Games and World Cups, or new national stadiums. They are not the priority. If Mr Bates and chums want a new national football stadium, let them pay for it themselves. It is ludicrous that a sport generating (and wasting) as much money as football should even be considered for Government assistance.

And while on the subject, if the Government feel it is necessary at this time to have a super stadium, for all sport and not just football, why throw money at Wembley? Why not build on a site accessible by road and rail instead of one that can be reached only by parachute or, if the customer is willing to take the risk, being fired in by a cannon? The present argument about how many spectators the new Wembley might hold is the biggest waste of time since the last meeting of the Flat Earth Society. The fact is a stadium taking 30,000 people would put an inordinate strain on the Wembley infrastructure, as anyone who has ever been there will tell you.

It is in the wrong place. It should be knocked down and sold for industrial development, which is all it is fit for. It is when you watch American sport and visit their stadiums you realise how unimaginative and backward we are, how enslaved by a so-called glorious past, how negligent of the future.

The reasons we are second to third rate are so obvious even politicians must see them clearly. Could it be that for all their fine words about sport, they don't really care?

November 1999

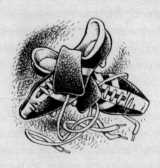

Life on the other side of the byeline

I said I was going to interview Garry Nelson. 'Garry who?' they said. We met in the foyer of a London hotel. He approached in the shy diffident manner of someone who does not expect to be recognised. He had come straight from playing for Charlton reserves against Tottenham's second team at an empty White Hart Lane.

That was the bad news. The good news was that his book is a bestseller. It is called *Left Foot Forward* and is sub-titled *A Year in the Life of a Journeyman Footballer*. It should be compulsory reading for any ambitious parent intent upon their son playing professional football. Every young player on the books of a professional club should study it and understand the difference between being Garry Nelson, soccer pro, and Alan Shearer, superstar.

Directors of football clubs, particularly the fat cats, should read the book to understand what life is like on the other side of the tracks. If, at the end of it all, someone does not hire Garry Nelson to promote the acceptable face of soccer, then the game is even more blinkered than I supposed it to be.

Nelson's idea was to set down a season in diary form, to explain what it is like to be a run-of-the-mill professional footballer. It does not have the wit or literary style of Eamon Dunphy's earlier book on life at Millwall

Football Club. Dunphy is both a romantic and a natural writer. Garry Nelson is neither. But in its own level-headed and straightforward way, his book is every bit as revealing.

Garry Nelson is in his seventeenth year as a professional footballer. He is nearing 700 league appearances and has scored more than 100 goals. He has played for Southend, Swindon, Plymouth, Brighton and Charlton. His most memorable moment was when Plymouth won promotion to the old Second Division. He has never been to Wembley and never played in the Premier League. On the other hand, he has never sniffed cocaine, taken a bung or jumped feet-first into the crowd.

He said, 'It seems soccer has capitulated to greed. Big money calls the shots. The personalities in the game now achieve celebrity status from their off-field antics. The press is full of drug taking, bungs, head-butting, kung-fu kicking. The mud flies in all directions and it sticks. We all suffer. So you are a footballer? Must be bent. That's what the public say. It's totally unfair to the vast majority of pros who are decent and hard-working.

'I hope the book manages to get this across. I think the people who run the game have to take a long hard look at what's happening. I think it will get worse before it gets better. There's so much money about nowadays and you wonder if anyone is really sitting down and working out how best it might be spent for the future of football.

'Once upon a time, we never knew who the directors were and the manager got on with managing a club. Today there are some very powerful people in the game and you begin to wonder what their real ambitions are. These are high-powered people used to having their own way and there seems little to stop them. They spend millions to survive in the Premier League. It seems the chairmen are saying let's make sure we're in it and forget about anyone else.

'But where does that leave Gillingham or Rochdale? I believe in a four-tier structure. I know something about it because I've spent my life working in it. I understand the importance of smaller clubs to their communities and to the structure of the game.

'Sooner rather than later I can see English soccer becoming more élite and synthetic than it is now. In my time as a pro, I have seen the gulf between the divisions widen drastically. I think that soon the rest of us will be told to bugger off. Then, no more local heroes, no more eleven good men and true. Sad.'

What the book illuminates with brutal clarity is the primitive ways clubs are run. Compared to directors of football clubs and their managers, the Borgias were paragons of enlightened man-management. Little wonder that at the bottom of this pyramid of intrigue the players are left to plot and scheme their own salvation. They live from contract to contract, scouring the back pages and even their own programme notes for indications of what the future might hold.

The fear of injury is ever present, the critic on the terrace the voice of doom. Tackled from behind last season at Bristol and knowing the injury was a bad one, Nelson was being carried off on a stretcher when a Bristol supporter leaned out from the terraces and shouted, 'That's your career over, you bastard. You'll never play again.'

He had much the same experience earlier in the season when he posed with a Charlton fan for a photograph. After he said cheese, he was approached by the photographer, the son of the fan, who said, 'You know, Nelson, you're useless nowadays. Rubbish. You ought to pack it in.'

Garry Nelson says that the footballer lives every day of his life with the question of what he will do when his career is over.

'I draw some consolation from the fact that several people who asked me that question – bank managers, for instance – who thought they were in secure jobs, are now out of work. Fact is nowadays no one is guaranteed a job for life.' He added, 'The advantage footballers have is that we grow up knowing that one day soon we will have to give up playing.

'It looks like the end of my career. I don't seem to be

in the reckoning at Charlton any longer. I think I have another couple of seasons left, but who's going to fork out for a player who is thirty-four going on thirty-five? Then there's the book. It's opinionated. I speak my mind. Therefore the judgement of another club taking me on might become more political than it would otherwise be.'

He has just passed a course in business management, runs a coaching school in America and owns a picture-framing business. He would like to work within the game. Perhaps Gordon Taylor might offer him a job. 'There's a lot to do. The game is fraught with problems,' Nelson said.

Football management? 'I always thought that one of the great joys of being a player was that it enabled me to see my children growing up. I don't think I'd want to sacrifice that to be a manager. The best a new manager can hope for is luck.

'When I signed for Swindon, Ken Beamish was the manager. He was superb at man-management, the best I've ever come across. He had been there a year, just signed a new contract, when they signed Lou Macari and Ken was gone. There's loyalty for you,' he said.

Garry Nelson did not hit it off with Macari. Swindon was the low point of his career. He joined Plymouth and that was the best of times.

'In the season we won promotion, we were on telly every week and in the papers every day. Because we were the only team in the West Country we were treated like real heroes. I knew for the first time what it must be like being a star.

'The players liked each other. There were no glamour-boys, no egos in conflict. It was the high point of my career. When I look back and perhaps wonder why I stuck it as a footballer, I recall those days at Plymouth and find the answer. Being part of a successful team, enjoying success and acclaim, being part of a community in that way is a fairly unusual experience. Not many people are given it.

'The reality, of course, comes later. That's Doncaster away on a cold and windy night when it's peeing down and you lose 2–0. The good thing is that in years to come when I'm retired and sitting with my mates in a pub yarning about the old days, it will be Plymouth and promotion we'll talk about. Bugger Doncaster,' he said.

It could be that during Garry Nelson's lifetime, eager young scholars will peruse his book searching for the lost tribes of English footballers who once existed when the game had ninety-two clubs in four divisions instead of six teams in a World Super League. All we can hope is that in the intervening years the people who play the game and those who run it will come to understand what he was trying to say. It is summed up by his first manager, Dave Smith, who told him, 'As a professional, always remember who you are, what you are and who you represent.'

Simple really.

December 1995

Garry Nelson retired as a player in 1997 aged thirty-six after a season as striker-cum-assistant manager with Torquay United. They finished 89th out of 92 league clubs, inspiring Nelson's second book, *Left Foot in the Grave*. He went on to work for the players' union, the Professional Footballers Association.

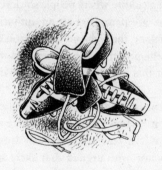

A THOROUGHLY
SHODDY TALE

IT WAS GOOD the Football Association reacted vigorously against those wretched ticket spivs at Leicester. It was sad, yet somehow typical, that the players and the officials of the club involved seemed unable to accept that what they had done was stupid and dangerous as well as greedy and repellent. They should be made to admit how crass they have been but it won't happen. They inhabit a culture where people shirk responsibility.

Footballers are pampered by an authority – the FA – good at making the right noises but too easily frightened off by the power of the players and the clubs. Let us hope that this tough stand is but the overture to a new era.

The game is in need of correction and control in so many areas it is difficult to know where to start. We could take as our text the statement from the guilty players' solicitor who argued that there had been no guidance to his clients about what to do with tickets. Have you ever heard such a pathetic, forlorn excuse in your life? The FA have probably not issued guidance to players about crossing the road, using a knife and fork, or wiping their bums. Does this mean they are disadvantaged to the point that if they walk in front of a bus it is the FA to blame?

Probably the answer is yes. Whatever happened to

good old common sense? Haven't players got a mind of their own, not to mention a conscience? Do they really want to spend their lives hiding behind lawyers and managers, weak-kneed club officials and cynical managers? Again, the answer is yes, which is why the FA really have to get stuck in.

Players apart, what about the role of the club in all this? What did they expect David Nish, the director of their Academy, to do with an allocation of 129 tickets? And if the man in charge of setting an example to young players ends up being fined £10,000 and adjudged not fit to handle tickets for another three years, what is the club going to do about that? Slap his wrist?

In fact, what the club did when it discovered that tickets used by fans involved in the day's disturbance had come from Andrew Impey's allocation was to fine him two weeks' wages. Steve Double, the FA spokesman, said that what should have been 'a pleasant day for many fans instead involved fear, intimidation and violence'. If you employed the man responsible, would you think docking two weeks' wages was sufficient punishment?

The behaviour of Leicester City Football Club in this inquiry has been one of the least attractive aspects of a thoroughly shoddy tale. The FA said their inquiry had been hindered by the club with a 'smoke-screen in certain areas'. That being the case, it is not just the players who should be clobbered but the club themselves. They should be charged with bringing the game into disrepute. That won't happen because by the very nature of their structure, the FA look after their own.

Adam Crozier, the new boy at the FA, seems eager for change. He has a tough ride ahead. I understand he has already been told that the FA is not a one-man show. But we should wish him well and hope he doesn't lose his nerve. The FA is the guardian of the game, not its poodle. Less yapping and more biting is what's needed, particularly of the hand that feeds it.

April 2000

MOANING MANAGERS ON THE WRONG SCENT

W HY THE FUSS about Attilio Lombardo and Tomas Brolin taking charge at Selhurst Park? Marc Goldberg is the boss and anyone prepared to pay £30 million for Crystal Palace obviously likes a gamble. Moreover, compared to his first idea of employing Messrs Venables and Gascoigne, giving the job to an Italian who doesn't speak English and a portly Swede with a face like a fallen cherub makes perfect sense.

I was interested that Harry Redknapp expressed surprise at Lombardo's appointment on the grounds of his inability to speak English. He must know that if fluency in the mother tongue was a pre-requisite, half the managers in the Premier League would be out of a job and the half who remained wouldn't all have been born in Britain.

That brings me, naturally enough, to Kenny Dalglish and something he said the other day about newspapers. He alleged they were fit only for accommodating dogs' droppings, or words to that effect. I presume he included in his condemnation the various tabloids he has taken money from during a long and lucrative career as a ghosted columnist.

I always think that football managers and players who call the media names are like people who hunt and refer to foxes as vermin. They should be aware that without the interest and enthusiasm of the media they despise, there would not be a game for them to be employed in. Furthermore, without the millions poured into the game by television, football managers would still be travelling to the game by bus thinking themselves lucky if they ended up with a newsagent's shop on the high street.

Mr Dalglish and his ilk should go down on bended knee every night and say a prayer for the preservation of the saintly Rupert. 'Dear Lord, may his cash flow never cease. Amen.'

In the culture of buck-passing and prevarication in football, it is either the media or the referees who are to blame for everything. Arsene Wenger thinks the time has come for video evidence to be allowed to assist the officials. Anyone who has heard the Arsenal manager claiming he didn't see the incident when one of his players misbehaved on the field will know his eyesight isn't what it should be and sympathise with someone so visually impaired as to need video evidence for that which most of us can see quite clearly with the naked eye.

His is a common complaint among football managers who have the eyes of a sparrowhawk in their opponents' penalty area but are afflicted with a terrible myopia in their own half of the field. So you might imagine they would be a bit more sympathetic to blind referees. Not a bit of it. Chelsea's Gianluca Vialli says referees have got it in for Dennis Wise. Diddums. Ian Wright is a marked man, a victim. Bless his cotton socks. David Batty is a pussy cat really. Bonny lad. It's the referees to blame for all the bookings. There ought to be two of them, one in each half of the pitch. Why stop there? Why not one for each player. Plus video evidence. That should do the trick.

The other suggestion is that whether there be one referee on the field or twenty-two, they should be drawn from the ranks of ex-players. They know what's what. They certainly do. It would be a bit like putting a wife beater in charge of a marriage bureau.

Why anyone would want to be a referee nowadays beats me. They are reviled, spat upon, cursed, terrorised, jostled and threatened. And that's what happens when they come through the junior leagues. When they reach the top of their profession, things get much worse. For what? The kind of money the modern player would consider loose change. They must be crackers. What is more, they are isolated in their misery. The FA does nothing, which is what the FA does better than most. They are much too busy bothering about the opinions of Señor Havelange and whither Wembley, which only reveals their enthusiasm for lost causes. Both are monuments to the game's past and, in my view, have nothing to do with the future. The same could be said, of course, about the FA.

Why should Wembley be so important to us securing a future World Cup? It might be the most famous football ground in the world but it's a long way from being the best. For one thing you can't reach it without allowing an extra day for travel and parking, and for another the purchase of a seat is not always the guarantee of a perfect view. I won't further detail the obvious shortcomings of plumbing designed for a different era when spectators could watch a match without first drinking ten pints of lager. Wouldn't it be better, more impressive, more significant, if we built a stadium people could travel to in style and occupy in comfort? I am talking about a proper football ground, not some shared facility with athletics and dog racing. It should be the best *football* stadium in the world and that would be something to boast about and something capable of luring a World Cup.

As it is, any claim we have for the future will depend not on what happens to Wembley but what happens in France. Any trouble with our hooligans – and who dare

bet against it – and Borneo would have a better chance of playing host.

How do we change the ugly faces on the terraces? Changing the ugly faces on the field and on the bench would be a good place to start. No one wants the game to lose its cutting edge but managers and players must begin to accept responsibility for what happens on the field of play. Blind referees and venal journalists have nothing to do with it. In the final analysis, they are mere witnesses. Fallible? Certainly. Culpable? Not unless you are frightened of the truth and are seeking a fall guy.

March 1998

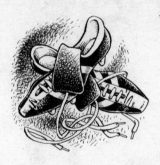

'When the seagulls follow the trawler, it is because they think
sardines will be thrown into the sea' – *Eric Cantona in answer
to questions about his demonstration of kung fu in April 1995*

'When we follow the trawler, it is because we think Eric is
speaking a load of codswallop' – *A flock of seagulls*

'When the great bootmaker in the sky looks down over Old
Trafford, he will see that Eric the Philosopher is a stud short of
a full set' – *Albert Camus*

ENVOI

This book is dedicated to the people who write about football – not all of them, but those who have stuck to their task remembering the adage there is no cheering in the press box.

The job of reporting the game is much more complicated nowadays. There was a time when the people who wrote about football had much in common with those who played it. It was an easy relationship. These days players are separated from reality by agents, accountants and smoked-glass windows. There are also too many ex players reporting the game.

I am not totally against ex pros being given access to the media. They can sometimes offer perceptive insights but more often they are too eager to turn a blind eye to players' indiscretions, ever willing to promote the image rather than the reality. The journalist, on the other hand, must be someone who loves the game while condemning its faults, who serves it by telling the truth as he or she sees it. It always was a job worth doing. Today it is as necessary as it is worthwhile.

To those sports writers who inspired me, including John Arlott and H.D. Davies, and to those I have been lucky enough to work alongside, particularly the talented team at the *Daily Telegraph* assembled by David

Welch, my thanks and admiration. To those who take up the challenge, I offer the hope they gain from the experience the joy and fulfilment I have had.